THE STUDENTS GUIDE TO AN EPIC ONLINE REPUTATION ...AND PARENTS TOO!

WAYNE DENNER

What Every Student needs to keep their
Reputation in Shape in a Digital World

SECOND EDITION

THE FUTURE

'Individual talent is becoming increasingly important in the 21st century. What one knows and can do with their knowledge in differing contextual formats drives their employability. In other words, people who can innovate and generate new value with their knowledge will lead employment growth. Those who do not will be replaced by machines, outsourced, or be outmoded by those who can (inspired by Clarke, 1980, p. 96)'.

Knowmad Society

KNOWMAD SOCIETY

"[...] a nomadic knowledge worker — that is, a creative, imaginative, and innovative person who can work with almost anybody, anytime, and anywhere. Industrial society is giving way to knowledge and innovation work. Whereas industrialization required people to settle in one place to perform a very specific role or function, the jobs associated with knowledge and information workers have become much less specific concerning task and place. Moreover, technologies allow for these new paradigm workers to work within broader options of space, including "real," virtual, or blended. Knowmads can instantly reconfigure and recontextualize their work environments, and greater mobility is creating new opportunities."

....

Moravec, 2008

"It takes 20 years to build a good reputation and five minutes to ruin it. If you think about that you'll do things differently."

....

Warren Buffett

BACK IN THE DAY

In the late noughties Wayne set up Ireland's First Social Networking Website.

Before Myspace, Facebook and Bebo. Yes Bebo. It's making a comeback you know ☺

He believes he could have been Mark Zuckerberg. But the banks weren't lending. They said social networking would never catch on...

NOTE TO PARENTS:

"I'm one too. Of two boys, aged 5 and 6. In less than 10 years I'll be giving them this book, (thanks Dad). Take it from me - teenagers need to read this book and books like it. The future has changed for job hunters. Personal Reputation and how they use technology is key to your child's future education, career and life opportunities. Your Kid's Online Reputation Matters."

himself@waynedenner

REVIEWS

'This book is an absolute 'must read' for every generation. For young people who live in a world where their CV is now their Online Presence it is vital to understand how they can be proactive in shaping their future. Whether it be getting into University or securing the perfect job, their Online Reputation matters. For parents, this knowledge is key to helping their children and understanding how Online Reputation affects the whole family. Wayne is particularly skilled in reaching all age groups and his passion for passing on his considerable knowledge makes this book very readable.'

Tracy Edwards MBE

"This is an energetically written book that will appeal to its target audience, and contains a wealth of important insights for teenagers and young adults to navigate their way through the digital landscape without causing themselves any embarrassment or distress at a later stage in life. There's an abundance of actionable tips for teenagers to take control of their own online presence, and Wayne doesn't shy away from the tough issues but engages with them head on. A must read for the digital native generation that's now coming of age."

Barry Adams - Polemicdigital.com

"Upbeat, fast-paced, packed with tips to make you look like an asset to your employer. Your Online Reputation Matters. A lot."

Belfast Telegraph

ISBN 978-0-9934815-0-5

Books may be purchased in quantity and/or special sales
by visiting waynedenner.com/books

Published by: 10th Step, Ltd, Warrenpoint, Northern Ireland
A catalogue entry of this book is available from the British Library

Second Edition
Printed in United Kingdom

CONTENTS

/STOP I THINK I POST

Good Day! And thanks for picking up this book, especially if you bought it with your hard earned part-time job money/money from your parents/EMA/Dole/ cash you found in street etc. I'm Wayne Denner, Digital Ninja Extraordinaire. Think of me as the parrot on your shoulder with Jedward-style hair reminding you that every time you post a Facebook status, send a Tweet, Share a Picture or Post-Anything-Online, you hear me squawking:

STOP I THINK I POST

Because that's the message I'll be banging on about throughout the book. Remember that, and you're done! In fact you can put the book down now. Only joking. Pick it back up, I've a few more squawks for you...

By reading this book cover to cover and then, once you finish it, passing it onto your bestie so they too can learn from the knowledge being handed out by the Digital Ninja, you're on the path to harvesting the true power the Internet holds... and most importantly - Using It To Your Advantage.

/THE UNSTOPPABLE INTERNET

Think about it. Today we're surrounded by smart phones. Now I'm not saying that's a bad thing (in fact, along with most of the world, my smart phone is my most treasured possession and definitely top of the list of 'things to be rescued first in a fire' (sorry kids).

They're absolutely everywhere. What's more, we're connected pretty much 24/7. Every one of us has a voice with a global reach, the power to create content and connect with millions of people all over the world. Fantastic. Right?

With the explosive growth of social media platforms and apps such as Facebook, Twitter, Instagram, Snapchat and Bebo (yes, Bebo – it's making a comeback you know), backed up by an endless number of websites on the Internet, our Online Reputation has never been more important. In fact everything we do in our daily lives can now be played out online, not just by us, but by others who are capturing content on our behalf. Whether we like it or not.

Some say we have no control of this out of control train...
Or do we? Yes! We Do. That's The Point of this Book!

Here's the thing - over 350 million pictures are uploaded to Facebook every day, with the average Facebook user uploading 217 photos apiece. Meanwhile Snapchat, a platform which has a much smaller user base than the mighty Facebook, is also getting 350 million snaps uploaded a day. And growing.

. . . .

"But Wayne" I hear you say.
"I'm only uploading a few pictures to Facebook and sending the odd funny Snapchat, though, OK, maybe some are a little un-PC/risqué/ inappropriate,"
"Do I really need to get hung up about my Online Reputation?"
Again. Yes. A Big Fat YES.

. . . .

/YOUR REPUTATION PRECEDES YOU!

Even if you've only had your picture taken once by a local newspaper (many of which now upload their content online) you have a digital footprint which needs managed.

Here's an even scarier fact for the digital generation. Babies and young children who've not even used a tablet or smart phone find themselves with a digital footprint, because proud parents are taking (a lot of) pictures and posting them on social media platforms. Thanks Mum and Dad!

For many of us, Social Media platforms have become the platform of choice for how we like to play out and share our lives.

On average, we spend 20 minutes per visit on Facebook. This works out at an average per user, per month of... clicks furiously on calculator app... 8.3 hours - that's a hell of a lot of time every month. Think of the amount of information we're uploading, sharing and commenting on. Then think about how it's contributing to our Online Reputation. And that's just time spent on Facebook, what about all the rest - Twitter, Snapchat, Instagram. Keeping up is like a full-time job. That nobody pays you for.

"Oh crap." I hear you say -
"I had no idea..." Well, now you do.

Everything you do and say online will have a positive or negative impact on your Online Reputation. So how are you going to keep yours in shape?

This isn't a reason to start hyperventilating, all is not lost. The good news is this book is here to give you tips on how to improve, protect and manage your Online Reputation. Some would go so far as to say (mainly me)(but not just me) that it's an essential read for anyone who uses social media, wants a decent job/lifestyle and lives on this planet.
Moving on...

"But," I hear you say, "Wayne, I don't have a clue what information is out there on the world wide interwebs. Where do I possibly start? Aaaaargghhhh!" One step at a time muchacho. We're getting to that part. I'm just thrilled you bought a copy of this book – well at least I hope you did (or begged, borrowed or stole it, doesn't really matter as long as you're reading it!) – it'll help you put your best foot forward, get yourself an Epic Online Reputation and keep it in shape.

Now are you ready? Sign out of FB and Twitter, put your smart phone on snooze, laptop to sleep etc etc. Let's begin...

/THE GOOD OUL DAYS BEFORE THE INTERWEBS

You probably can't remember a time when the Internet wasn't around. In fact, I can only just about remember a time when there was no Internet - yes it's true, I am still under 35 (just).

Before the Internet, Reputation was a very important aspect of people's lives. Back then, they spent years building it and developing relationships around it. In fact, many businesses were built on it and people spoke of that business as having a 'great reputation' or 'don't go near that shop, they have a reputation for serving rat meat as chicken'. (A very extreme example. Don't fret).

Many small town shops only survived because of the great relationships they'd developed with their customers – children would shop in the same stores as their parents did back in the day, all because of these connections and the reputation the business had.

If you think about it, back then, when the world really was a smaller place, those relationships were stronger than the ones which many of us develop now. Aw come on, you've only known that guy on FB for five minutes.

That being said, true relationships – both on and offline – take time to develop and need to be nurtured. In the age of the Internet and Social Media, relationships which have taken years to develop can be damaged in just a few minutes. The speed of the internet and the spread of information – much of which takes place in a real time environment – can damage even the best of businesses beyond repair. So just think about what it can do to your Personal Reputation.

This book has been written with YOU in mind - the ideas I'm sharing are a series of steps and processes to keep you ahead of the posse. And to minimise the risks of you damaging your life by posting or sharing something you'll live to regret or that will haunt you for a long long long long long time. (Note to Ed; maybe too many longs. They get it)

/THE WAY WE MAKE FIRST IMPRESSIONS WITH PEOPLE IS ONLINE

From now on, I want you to think about absolutely everything you post online, who can see it and what impression it leaves.

STOP | THINK | POST

What about your current employer – if they came across your post what would they think? You've heard the saying if you wouldn't want your grandma to hear or see it, perhaps you shouldn't post it online. Think of your boss in the same way.

When it comes to Online Reputation, many people don't think about it as something which can open and close doors. Well I'm here to tell you that it can. And it does.

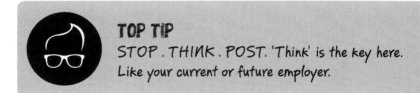

TOP TIP
STOP . THINK . POST. 'Think' is the key here.
Like your current or future employer.

/NOTE TO SELF: DIGITAL DIRT STICKS

Check out the Orange video on Youtube
(https://www.youtube.com/watch?v=JJfw3xt4emY)

According to Mashable (from as far back as 2011) 90% of recruiters will check you out online and 50% will screen you out based on information they find online. What's even more interesting/scary is that 87% of college recruiters now admit to carrying out online searches on potential applicants.

'Nearly all (93%) of recruiters are using LinkedIn to discover talent. This is up from 87% in 2011 and 78% in 2010. Furthermore, 89% of recruiters have hired through LinkedIn'.

....

Time/Business Time.com (2012)

Now, for many reading this book, it may seem like the social media age has been around years and the Internet forever. Although many students have never known life without social media or the Internet, it's actually not that old (cue your parents banging on about the 'old days' when mobile phones were 'bricks' you could only phone or text on, and social networking was restricted to meeting their friends in the pub...). With the Internet rapidly growing, people are still coming to terms with how it works and what the pitfalls are, of which there have been many.

Paris Brown was the successful applicant who became the UK's first Youth Police Commissioner at just 17 years old. But after only a short spell in the job, the media dug up inappropriate tweets she'd posted when she was just 14. They jumped on this, making her role untenable and forcing her to resign after just a few weeks, in a role which would have opened the door to connections for life, all around the world. And with it, she had to give up a salary of £15,000 per year.

The thing to remember about the Interwebs and Social Media platforms is they are like an elephant. They store and remember everything and, as a result, you need to be totally on the ball when using both. And this is where I come in. To help, think of me, if you will, as your Digital Ninja.

I'm going to show you how to Kung Fu kick the life out of anything negative online.

"How?" I hear you say.
Well, by living by the Golden Rule of STOP |THINK|POST.

THINK! Would you be happy with your future children seeing these images or messages. "But Wayne I'm only a teenager and have no plans to have children for a very long time." I'm glad to hear that. But guess what? Content on the Interwebs can be around for a lifetime. It's here to stay and you need to start thinking about anything you post online from this moment on. The past is the past. It's out there but we can help protect your Online Rep moving forward.

OK, have I got your attention? Let's roll up our sleeves.

/BACK IN THE DAY

It's hard to believe that the internet as we know it has only been around for 25 years - and it's just 10 years since the birth of Facebook. Facebook and other Social Network platforms have become a central part of how we like to share and receive information. Many people no longer send emails opting for Facebook message or apps as their preferred method. There were, of course platforms before Facebook, and the Internet was around long before Facebook.

Let's step back and think about life before Facebook. Back when I started out on the Internet, it was a very different place. AOL – or AOHell as I used to call it – was my service provider. Yes Sir - cue that pesky dial up sound (googles dial up sound). With Yahoo as the search engine of choice, I don't even remember Google being around back then. Now, if we want to find absolutely anything out what do we do? We ask Google. Back in the early days it might have been Ask Jeeves (though I think this might be still going) – go on, Google 'Ask Jeeves'.

In the early days of the Internet no one gave any thought to Online Reputation and the impact that it might have on our future career or how it could affect a person's chance of getting a job or a place at uni. Now everything we post, share and say online is adding to our digital record. Mistakes which we make today can be searchable tomorrow and forever.

Back in the day in my college we had just three computers in the library (I hear you gasp). You had to queue to get on them and your allocated time was a maximum of 15 minutes per session. As it took 20 minutes to dial up (google Dial up sound again. Painful memories), internet use was limited to the relentless few, (of which of course, I was one).

Nowadays, every student has their own laptop, tablet or smart phone. Some have all three. The thing is, when I made mistakes when I was younger – and believe me, I made my fair share, as did everyone else – there was no digital camera to capture them and no Facebook or Twitter to upload and share them.

Suddenly everyone's armed with a HD camera and access to more channels to share information on than a seasoned CNN reporter.

When it comes to the Internet - just because we can, doesn't mean it's a good idea. When it comes to doing silly things online we're our own worst enemies, creating content and uploading it without a second thought. But it's not just young people who've been caught out. There have been judges, celebrities and even mature(?!) media-trained politicians who have fallen on their social media sword. We'll come back to this later.

You're probably sitting there thinking, "But Wayne, I only send the odd email and I'm not even on Facebook, Twitter or anything. Do I still need to think about my Online Reputation?" Yessirree Bob, you certainly do. Everything's online now. Even if you've only had your picture taken by the local newspaper and you featured in the article or in press releases, there's a very good chance that you'll be mentioned somewhere online – it's better you know where before someone points it out to you.

You see, as the Internet and Social Media grow, they're very hard to avoid. Your best bet is to put steps in place and understand how you can protect your Online Reputation.

/READY, STEADY...

"OK – enough. Tell me how I can become a Digital Ninja like you – or a Jedi Master or whatever – and keep my Online Reputation in shape."
Well my friend, I can tell you that the training is not going to be easy but if you take part, you'll reap the benefits when your next employer searches you Online, or you start your next relationship, or you apply for that place at uni.

...GO!

Like everything we do in life, being in the right mind-set is important. The journey which we're about to embark on requires change. Change to developed behaviours and habits which are the result of not paying enough attention to what we posted, shared and said online. I mean, when we started out we wouldn't have thought it would come back to haunt us. Or that, as I mentioned earlier, 93% of recruiters would be using Social Media and the Internet to check us out online, or that 50% would screen us out based on what they found.

That alone begins to put things in perspective. Last year the marketing analyst firm On Device Research reported 'one in 10 young job seekers lost a job opportunity because of their social media profiles' (Job.aol). What's on Facebook, Twitter, and other platforms can stop you being hired. And can get you fired. I kid you not.

TOP TIP
Google Yourself. But not in a needy way ☺ Do this every few weeks and definitely before a potential employer looks you up.

Now I'm going to throw down the gauntlet and put it out there – the way that we apply for jobs over the next five years is going to change – in fact scrap that, it already has changed. What I'm seeing now is a fundamental shift in how employers are hiring people and advertising jobs and opportunities – it's all moving online. You're not going to buy a newspaper to look for jobs – that was how our parents used to do it. Most positions are now advertised directly on an employer's website, newspapers online or recruitment portal – hell, I'd go so far as saying that eventually CVs will become a thing of the past. It's already started, with many people now focusing on building and developing their LinkedIn Profiles as a sort of digital CV, but one where others can endorse their skills and leave recommendations. Similar to how references used to work.

The whole game plan for advertising and applying for jobs is changing as a direct result of the Internet and Social Media and I have no doubt that it will continue to evolve this way.

One major reason why our Online Reputation is something we need to protect is because it'll influence the college or uni you'll get in to (or not) as well as the job you get (or don't get), which will ultimately define your career and lifestyle.

Obviously guys this will have an impact on the girl/boy you end up with. You know what I mean here.

Because of the growth of platforms such as LinkedIn, there's a very high chance that when you leave school or university you'll be using it (or something similar that hasn't been invented yet) to look for your next job, or at least build your professional network. This is an area we're going to explore later in the book.

/TAKING CONTROL OF YOUR ONLINE REPUTATION

'You have to assume that online reputation is always checked'.

Dennis O'Neill (Executive Coach)

Before we dive into the world of how to protect your Online Reputation, it's important to take a few steps back and get a definition as to what Online Reputation really is. Exact definitions differ but one around Reputation from good ol' Wikipedia states:

"Reputation management is the understanding or influencing of a individual's or businesses reputation."

Mmm. Could be better.

Just on this point, I like Techopedia's practical advice on taking control of your Reputation, 'using positive material to counteract, balance or "push" negative material. An example is using online content to influence Google's search engine results pages'.

For the purposes of this book, we're looking at it from all things Online and Social Media and how it can impact or hinder your future career and life opportunities.

I like to keep it 'simples' and would define it as 'Everything you do and say online and on your mobile will impact your Online Reputation'.

Just so there's no confusion.

/YOUR ONLINE REPUTATION IS EVERYTHING YOU - OR SOMEONE ELSE - CREATES ABOUT YOU ONLINE

If we think about it, before the Internet it was a lot easier to control what people said about us and protect our Reputation. Now we just do a quick search on Google to find someone or Google ourselves. (I do it all the time. But not in a needy way. ☺. This reveals first impressions – and these can be both positive and negative about a person's character and Reputation. My handy sketch below shows potentially all the channels, which could have an impact on your Reputation or Digital Tattoo.

This example is, of course, a simplified doodle but you can see pretty easily how, with all those digital channels (and possibly future ones which haven't been invented yet), this can turn into a whole lot of information out there about you – some which you're not even aware of. Additionally content which others are creating on your behalf could be impacting your own Online Reputation and, like it or not, most people will judge you based on the first impressions they find online or on your profile. Without even having met you. That includes college and job recruiters.

/BIGGEST THREAT ONLINE = YOU

I can't say this too many times - it's Extremely Important that you take care online. There are bad people out there. People who'll prey on you when you're feeling vulnerable or lonely. Sad but true. You need to be aware of this and keep yourself and your friends safe. BUT. When it comes to your life and career, it's all down to you my friend.

YOU. ARE. YOUR. NO1. THREAT.

This may come as some sort of surprise but - Your Biggest Threat Online is You, i.e. you uploading something, which you later regret.

/THE SECRET FORMULA TO ONLINE REPUTATION SUCCESS

Big fanfare and drumroll build up...

/THERE IS NO SECRET FORMULA

'Oh', I hear you say above the deafening silence of a big anti-climax. 'Then why are you wasting my time?' Please stick with me here. As I said, there is no secret formula or magic which can offer you Online Reputation Success. But there are a few simple steps which I've found to be effective in protecting your Online Reputation, help you keep your Digital Tattoo on track and keep you ahead of the game in a competitive digital world.

STEP #1
/ KNOW WHAT THE SEARCH ENGINES KNOW ABOUT YOU

/GOOGLE YOURSELF!

But remember not in a needy way ☺.

You should start your search on the world's most popular search engine. Think about how many times a day we use it to ask questions and find answers. It has changed the way we access information forever. With just a click of a mouse.

If you've never done it before, open Google, type your name in, press enter and see what results are returned. Take yourself through the first 10 pages of Google and actively click on links which might be directly connected to you – of course there might be others out there in Cyberspace with the same name – but if you come across something make a note of it and how it was created.

I can hear you thinking. 'That was easy. That's it I'm done. Now I know what's out there about me, I can go get pizza'. But hold the pizza for a minute. You haven't been as thorough as you thought. What you need to do now is carry out the same search, this time looking for images and see what results are returned.

Then... it may seem like it sometimes, but Google isn't the only search engine in the world, so it might be worth your while having a quick search on some of the others for example:

YAHOO / BING / ASK / AOL / MYWEBSEARCH / WEBCRAWLER / BLEKKO / DOGPILE / DUCKDUCKGO / ALHEA / INFO /CONTENKO

It's just possible that each of these search engines may have different results, so it's better to take a quick look and see what they show too.

Now I do have some good news. Well actually two bits of good news. First, this will really help you become more aware of potential issues around any negative stuff which may be floating about on the Interwebs about you, so at least you know about it before a potential employer comes across it and points it out to you (red face avoidance).

The second thing is, the search engines are constantly crawling the Internet seeking new information and results to rank, so carrying out this search once a year is probably not going to do you any favours. If you can, I'd suggest doing it once a month.

/ALERT STATUS

You should also set up a Google Alert. It's simple to use and will alert you via email when any new or interesting content appears, depending on what you want it to search for. Some people use it to track sports teams and pop stars, but you should also input your own name – that way, if anyone posts anything about you, you'll be alerted to it automatically, helping you stay in control of your Online Tattoo. I suggest you take yourself across to http://www.google.com/alerts and try it out. Especially if a potential employer is on the radar. Thank me later.

Note: It helps if you put your name in quotation marks, like so: "wayne denner". This will ensure Google only shows results with the full name in it. Without quote marks, you'll see results for people called 'wayne' and other people with the 'denner' surname. Same applies to setting up a Google alert - make sure you use quote marks, otherwise you'll get a lot of notifications for people who only share one part of your name!

STEP #2
/ PRIVACY IS KEY

/KEEP YOUR PERSONAL INFORMATION PRIVATE.

When it comes to keeping stuff private online, it's harder than you think. It's up to you to remember to adjust the privacy settings accordingly to what you're posting online and who you'd like to view and potentially share with. Online and Mobile privacy can be somewhat difficult to achieve – yes, of course, platforms do offer settings to update privacy, but they vary from platform to platform and are not always the easiest to implement. This means it can be a complicated business at times and there's still a bit of concern about achieving privacy. If you use mobile apps for social networking – which I'm sure you do – you'll need to visit the privacy settings, as it's likely they'll be different to your more traditional web-based platform.

It's no secret that many of the platforms themselves have, at some point, fallen victim to scams which happen regularly online. This is another reason why, as users, we need to look for ways to increase our privacy settings.

According to Marketing Charts, 18-24 year olds on Facebook boast an average of 510 friends. Now I don't know about you, but I reckon there's a good chance that the people you call 'Friends' on Facebook aren't actually close buddies. So even if you have your privacy settings set, are you really happy sharing your information with them? They could be someone you maybe met just a couple of times. How much would you like them to know? Probably not as much as they're seeing. In the words of Robin and Pharrell "I hate those blurred lines. You know you wanna, you know you wanna. Hey hey hey." Cue Miley Twerking. I'm twerking. So catchy! Sorry.

TOP TIP
Use 'quote marks' when setting up your Google Alert!
Or you'll end up looking through thousands

OK. Now here's yet another thing to look out for, privacy settings are constantly changing – from the fine print to the features which control them – so you need to be aware of just how they work and how you can update your settings should the network or platform make any tweaks to them. Keeping your information private online is not always easy – the only real way to keep your information safe is to lock it up or keep it in your head.

"But that isn't very practical Wayne I hear you say."

I KNOWWWWW!!!

It doesn't matter which Social Networks you're using, when it comes to your privacy it's important that you ask yourself:

- » Who can view my profile?
- » Who can see my posts?
- » What information am I sharing with external sites and businesses?
- » What applications can access my data?
- » Can my 'friends' share this information about me?
- » Is my location being shared?

TOP TIP

When sorting privacy settings check out your mobile apps too as they may be different to your web applications. And they change a lot. Review regularly.

STEP #3
/ WE LOVE TO SHARE

Way too many of us are sharing absolutely everything going on in our lives via social media. Come on guys!

Would you share that picture of you doing something dumb at work? Would you share that status about that nightmare customer who caused you lots of hassle at work recently? Should you post and allow others to share that your Boss is an a***? Not a great career move.

Hm, thought that. But you know what? It's the dumb things which we share on the Internet and Social Media which get us into the most trouble. As I mentioned earlier the Interweb never forgets and to get information removed is *EXTREMELY* hard and sometimes impossible. Did I mention that before? I think I did.

When it comes to sharing on Social Media we all have different reasons. Research carried out by The New York Times Psychology of Sharing has revealed the reasons why we do it:

- » Value and Entertainment 94%
- » Promote Causes 84%
- » Nourish Relationships 78%
- » Self-fulfilment 69%
- » Define Identity 68%

Google CEO Eric Schmidt said that the Internet 'needs a delete button and the lack of a delete button is a significant issue.' How right was he? Sadly no such button exists. Therefore everything we share can become associated with the sort of person that we may or may not be.

Furthermore by sharing or posting something online, you could also be incriminating yourself legally with police Services around the world who are now using footage from platforms such as YouTube to bring perpetrators to justice. An example of this was in 2011 during the Vancouver Stanley Cup riots, Police used videos uploaded by other people at the scene to track down, charge and prosecute people of acts of vandalism and disorderly conduct. Custodial sentencing resulted – Yes from YouTube videos.

When you share something via social media you have no idea who can see it or what consequences it may have not only for you but also for the other people who've shared it. When we share something, most of us think of the people within our network who can see it and not about the others outside your network who can also see it. This becomes a major concern when sharing images and videos online because of how easily these days stuff can go viral. Once this happens you risk losing complete control of who's seeing it and where it ends up.

TOP TIP

Grab a bright light and interrogate yourself. Questions listed on P33 will start you off.

/A VIRAL LESSON

In 2013, a fifth grade teacher wanted to teach her students about digital privacy, so she photographed herself holding a message. The photo went viral. It was shared nearly 500 times from the original post before it was reposted to a second fan page, Society's Choice, where it got more than 22,000 shares.

Cumulatively, it got more than 800,000 likes. But was that the end?
Of course not.

The photo found its way onto Reddit where it received more than 900 comments. That must be the end I hear you say. Wrongo! Someone taking part in the r/photoshopbattles (a sub-reddit for people to create new images) decided to take it another step further by showing how easy it was to edit and change the content of the photo's message. This ensured the photo was kicking around for a long time afterwards and still being shared, but without the original message.

TOP TIP
Don't be afraid to ask your friends to un-tag you.
You won't thank them if you lose out over that 'hilarious'
Saturday night pic...

STEP #4
/PAY ATTENTION TO WHAT YOU'RE TAGGED IN

Unwanted tagging in posts, pictures, tweets and other online content can be a massive problem for many people. For those doing the tagging, it's probably seen as a bit of fun. But I've seen all too many times the issues this can cause, not to mention the stress. The very nature of tagging is a minefield. And difficult to control. For example on your Facebook page, everyone on your friends list can see it – like the time my mum uploaded a pic of me when I was five in my Spider Man outfit. Needless to say it was shared - a lot. By my 'friends'. Thanks Mum.

It can become even more of an issue when other people tag you in unrelated pictures or videos, just to get the content onto your page which means all your friends can see it. Then it won't be long before someone at school, college or work comes across it. What do you think it'll do to your Online Reputation? Do you know how much damage it could potentially cause you if a future employer was to see it?

If you find yourself tagged in a picture on Facebook which you are not happy about, un-tag it straight away. If it surfaces again, contact the person doing the tagging and ask them, nicely, to stop. If it appears again with you tagged in, contact Facebook by simply reporting the image in the Report/RemoveTags (go to your Timeline / View Activity Log / Photos. Click the box on left of the offending photo, then Report/Remove Tags). Sorted.

STEP #5 /GENERATE POSITIVE CONTENT

The Ultimate Online Reputation Tip: Become an Online Influencer
Moving forward, generating positive content will become the best way to make sure your Reputation online is seen in a positive light.

Lots of positive content can also help push any negative stuff further down the rankings – but be warned, generating positive content needs to be across all social media platforms and online channels.

Social media and the Internet provide massive opportunities for you to create your own unique content. But the difficulty here is knowing what will work and what won't so you need to be aware of how others will perceive it.

For instance, when it comes to applying for a job or that place in college, you want to know that if you're searched online, what will be returned will be results based around the positive content which you've created.

Don't be put off by the thought of creating content - it can be as simple as writing an short blog or article around the career which you want to get into. For example, if you want to become a space scientist, start creating content all around this. Share this content via your networks on Facebook, Twitter and LinkedIn. Engage with others of a similar mind and reply to content they post online - add comments on other users' blogs. It won't be long before this content is picked up via the search engines and connected back to you. Just think how impressed your future employer or college will be if they come across your informed comments. And this will have the additional benefit of contributing towards your subject knowledge. And help blast off your future career as a space scientist. (Do you see what I did there?)

/DOES THE INTERNET HAVE MORE REACH THAN SMALL TOWN GOSSIP?

The short answer is, you guessed it - Yes, it does. Think about gossip in your town. How it spreads like wildfire. Well guess what. The Internet is X zillion times worse especially if something negative makes its way online about you, and the number of people who can see it is global. *Awwwwkward!*

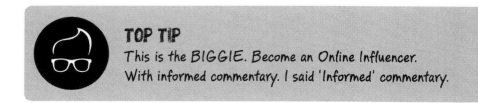

TOP TIP
This is the BIGGIE. Become an Online Influencer.
With informed commentary. I said 'Informed' commentary.

Gossip is an age old problem, but what many people seem to forget is that when it happens online, it can have very dangerous outcomes. For example if one of the major search engines were to pick up on gossip relating to you and other smaller search engines and directories were to pick this up and index it - well then the result multiplies, making it more difficult for you to remove this. In fact to remove it completely is near impossible.

So now you're thinking that small town gossip before the Internet doesn't seem so bad right? Right. The thing about gossip offline is that after a while, people get bored of it, it becomes yesterday's news and eventually dies out. But with the Internet, information has a habit of surfacing and being 're-shared' making it something which may never go away. Chillaxed times with a few drinks thrown in are a prime example of times to avoid the HD camera. Put them away guys. Anyway have you never heard of living in the moment?

NB Those on holiday and at festivals/nightclubs/house-parties take note. Way back in 2009, a study conducted by University of Massachusetts in co-operation with the US National Association of College Admission Counselling, found that colleges used social media for different purposes. It surveyed approximately 500 admission offices at accredited schools across the US and found that 29% of them used social networking platforms. These statistics present an interesting insight from as far back as 2009, showing that even back then social media played an important role in how schools reach their target communities. You have been warned!

/BECOMING A DIGITAL NINJA

When I was younger I loved watching Ralph Macchio. 'Who the hell's Ralph Macchio when he's at home?' I hear you ask. OK. Let's try another, Daniel LaRusso… no? OK, how about The Karate Kid? Oh yeah that movie with Mr Miyagi and the crane kick. Now you're with me, though you're probably wondering what has all this has got to do with Online Reputation.

Well I loved the Karate Kid movie so much I decided to take karate lessons. They lasted all of about three sessions because I couldn't pick it up fast enough.

So I decided to quit. Result.
I didn't become the Karate Ninja I dreamed of being.
I know I may seem random but here's the point.

Becoming a Digital Ninja and learning the skills to protect your Online Reputation and manage your Digital Tattoo, like karate, takes time but investing in the learning part does return results (do you get the Ninja part now?), especially when it comes to:

» Securing life and career opportunities,
» Building your own personal brand online
» Protecting your Online Reputation.

To date I've been able to leverage off the back of the technology which social media platforms have offered, to not only build my own personal brand but also turn something I love to do into a career and actually get paid... yes, paid! And you know what. It's not that hard. I mean, if I can do it, you can.

As the Internet evolves – and as yet it's only a 25 year old – it'll open up new opportunities for people – you! – to tap into. Most businesses now, if not all, have to have some sort of online marketing strategy in order to do business in today's economy. If you don't have a website, you're losing customers. Think about it like this – when was the last time you looked up a businesses number in the Yellow Pages? 'What's a Yellow Pages?' I hear you say. Well, in the olden days it was a big yellow book we used to look up telephone numbers of businesses. Yeah I know. Prehistoric!

The point I'm trying to make is that with all the new and exciting platforms and marketing channels popping up all the time, we now have access to a global audience. Yes. Even you. Who knows, maybe you'll come up with the next Instagram and Facebook might just buy it off you for a cool Billion Dollars!!

Whatever way you look at it, the Internet provides opportunities. You can use it for good, to get ahead, spread positive messages... or not. The choice is yours.

/START TAKING CONTROL

As a Digital Ninja, you need to not only start taking control of the content other people are creating about you, but also the content which isn't helping other people's Online Reputation (i.e. Your Friends). 'But Wayne, why should I care about what content others are creating?' It's all about Karma – if you Like/ Favour/Share/whatever posts about other people, that tiny mouse click can also have an impact on how your next potential employer views you.

Whether we like it or not, people can – and will – make assumptions about the type of person we are, based on things we've Liked online. Which is why you need to start taking control of any content which may be connected with you. Once you're in control, pass it on – help influence others around you to start thinking about the content they're creating and how it can have a direct effect on them.

When it comes to the Internet and Social Media, there are a whole host of websites and platforms where content can be created and content is hiding in the form of text, videos, comments, reviews... the list goes on. So what setting up alerts (as we discussed earlier) helps you find out about are their existence, but that may not be enough.

Remember search engines are like spiders on the interwebs (don't worry, not real ones arachnophobes). They love crawling the web for new content. Use this to help you take control and secure all of your digital profiles. I'm not going to list them here, but think about the main platforms which you are using on a daily basis. That being said, every day sees new platforms being launched, so part of Taking Control is also being aware of new stuff in the digital world.

You should assume that if you have a profile on any platform, it'll create a result in the search engines - not always the case, but it does happen a majority of the time. By Taking Control, you're starting to think in the past tense and become aware of what may have been posted or shared in the past. For example, what other content might there be out there about me – it could have been created by myself or others. A good starting point for this could be looking on the biggest social networking platform, Facebook, and checking your Activity Log. Your Activity Log will show all of your behaviour on Facebook and can allow you access to un-Liking of pages in one central location. It's handy.

/THINK LIKE YOUR NEXT EMPLOYER

'In today's job market, it's not enough to have the right education, experience, and qualifications: now, a great online reputation is another essential for job seekers to bring to the table'

Jessica Merritt, Reputation Management Expert
(Do hiring managers care about your online reputation? July 2014)

We've seen the stats about how many employers are now using Social Media and the Internet to screen potential job candidates.

'Ultimately, searching for candidates online is considered part of due diligence in today's market, whether or not it's fair to the candidate' Andrea Berkman (The Constant Professional).

Personally I think it's a great thing because it allows you to put yourself one step – if not more – ahead of those candidates who aren't using it to their advantage. The process of starting to think like your next employer can start when you're in school. In fact this is the best place to start your training to become a Digital Ninja.

The surge of employers and recruiters using Social Media to background check applicants (71% of recruiting organisations predict increasing their social networking search usage in 2014), actually opens up lots of exciting new ways for you, as the potential employee, to rise the top of your dream career in a online environment. That got you thinking didn't it! Keep reading…

You're in high school now and you're starting to think about what it is you might want to do when you leave – yes, I was there once too you know. You've lots of ideas, maybe you want to go on to University or College or maybe you already know what job you want to get in to or business you'd like to start. Whatever you decide, start using the Internet to your advantage by creating content around your job industry.

The best place to start is by Blogging - this is one of the most effective ways of generating what I call 'Positive Online Content' and you know what, Employers Love It! And not just them but Search Engines do too. It's one of the best ways to contribute towards your Online Reputation. You can be sure that the more results you have rattling around on the Internet, the better chance you have of future employers having more of a reason to invite you for an interview with their organisation. Prepare to be hunted down!

/WHATEVER YOU WANT

'What someone has on the world wide web often says just as much, if not more, about their professionalism and personality'.

....

Chaz Pitts-Kyser (Author - Careeranista)

Today's employers are looking for employees who can add real value to their business, someone who's constantly challenging the status quo (in a good way!), and who's always developing their own knowledge by aiming to be an expert in their field, and contributing to their industry. Positive Online Content can show them you're the right person for the job!

TOP TIP
Be aware of what is connected with you. And help your friends do the same. Your Activity Log on fb lets you do this in one handy spot!

/BUILD YOUR DIGITAL NETWORK

The growth of platforms such as LinkedIn has enabled users to develop a network of connections on a global basis. LinkedIn is the preferred platform for many recruiters acting on behalf of employers to source the best staff. Since its launch, the platform which I call the FacebookForYourCareer, currently has 3 million business pages... and is still growing. So this is one space you should focus your efforts on developing. As I see it, this shift from the way jobs would have traditionally been advertised (i.e. only in newspapers and the trade press) isn't only taking place on jobsites and company websites, it's also going on on LinkedIn.

Say you're considering becoming a top lawyer. Just think about this for a moment - the percentage of Top 50 US Law Firms that have a LinkedIn page is... 100%! Remember YOUR Digital Network helps you find jobs and helps employers find you.

/CRINGE!

You really, really, really – and I cannot emphasise this enough – do NOT want to post any embarrassing status updates on LinkedIn.

Platforms such as LinkedIn have allowed users to focus specifically on the career aspect of their Social Media, with many of the top global firms now opting to advertise their positions via the Internet and in particular on LinkedIn. The platform allows users to develop connections which are perhaps similar to Facebook friends, but not in the same context. As a user you can request what LinkedIn call 'Endorsements', which are basically recommendations - what job seekers before the Internet would have called references.

One great feature – which I really love about LinkedIn – is its ability for you to connect with others via connections which you already have. For example, one of your connections may be connected directly with someone in a company you'd like to work with – all you have to do is ask for what LinkedIn calls 'an introduction' and you could be 'in'. Pretty cool eh!

LinkedIn offers real value in terms of search engine visibility. If you've taken the time to properly update your profile, it should appear higher up in the rankings when someone searches your name on Google - which is B.I.G. in terms of adding creditability to your Online Reputation. Look at this as your Online CV if you will.

As you build your network of connections on the platform, you'll also get the opportunity to join and contribute to any of the 2.1 million discussion groups - many about specific career paths. Joining these groups will give you the chance to expand your network, resulting in being presented with even more opportunities. All from the comfort of your bedroom/living room/bedsit/café/bar.

So I reckon you must be loving all this Digital Ninja training, right? Let's stealthily move on...

/IT'S ALL ABOUT ME!

LinkedIn isn't the only platform out there you can use to build your career network on. You could be looking to all of the platforms to help build your digital network. Another great thing to do is set up your about.me page which basically acts like your business card on the web - another listing with good visibility which tells a little about you, what you're about and how people can reach you.

/JOB HUNTING IN THE DIGITAL AGE

A JOB COMES A KNOCKING...

'It's essential for job seekers to develop a positive online reputation - or at least wipe out any major red flags that might spell trouble' Reputation Management

Throughout this book I've been talking about the platforms and the tools you can use to positively approach and boost your opportunities of getting the job you want. When it comes to the Internet and your next big opportunity I believe anything is possible #TrueDat

There has been an explosive growth in usage of platforms such as LinkedIn in relation to how they have become the 'Facebook for your Career.' LinkedIn have 300 million members in over 200 countries and territories (the UK having 15M members alone). In 2012, members used LinkedIn for over 5.7 billion professionally-oriented searches on the platform. Now it doesn't take a genius me (☺) to work out that this could well be something that's worth investing time, in if you want to get your profile recruiter or employer-friendly.

Now earlier I shared some tips and advice on how you can work at getting an *All Star Profile* – so if you've skipped over that part of the book (if you did, I will look for you, I will find you, and I will make you read it), believe me it's worth going back for a read or reread.

'Now stop rambling Wayne and trying to come up with clever lines from the movie Taken and get to the point. Tell us what opportunities you've had from the Interwebs.'

JOB HUNTING IN THE DIGITAL AGE

Well, back in late 2013 I was spending time creating content around new and emerging social media platforms and apps, and researching just how businesses could get more value out of using them to engage with customers – especially those who could be reached based on their geo-location.

The whole aspect of location-based marketing really fascinates me because it's all so new (I mean, skip back 20 years and all marketeers had at their disposal was TV, Print or Radio, all of which had a massive price tag attached). I started sharing content via LinkedIn, mainly tweeting and contributing to a number of blogs as a guest contributor and sharing my thoughts and insights.

TOP TIP
Keep Linkedin 'clean' and career focussed.
Dont be tempted to share any private thoughts here.

It wasn't long before, totally out of the blue, I received an email from a recruiter for a well known global brand. The message was vague - along the lines of 'a position within the company had just been created and they wanted to discuss some of the content which I'd created and how it impacts brands such as theirs'. It went on to ask would I be free at some point for a quick phone call chat.

As I'm a massive fan of networking and building relationships online and off, I sent them a reply back with my contact details and some suggested dates when I'd be free to talk, then thought nothing more about it.

About a week or so later I was driving to Belfast for a meeting when my phone rang. I answered it – using my hands free of course. The person on the other end introduced themselves as the lead recruiter for said global brand – I think to start with I sounded rather strange as I'd actually forgotten I'd arranged the telephone call with them. Nevertheless I was excited and we chatted for 15 minutes or so about my background and experience in the area of digital marketing. They were particularly interested in my thinking on how a major global brand such as theirs could become a more socially connected brand using mobile platforms to engage with their audience. Now anyone who knows me knows how excited I get with mobile apps! I'm always the first to try out new platforms and figure out how people and businesses can maximise use out of them. Off the top of my head, I came up with some ideas and examples of how I saw this aspect of business communication developing and the positive benefits as I saw them. We wrapped up our call and the recruiter said they'd feed things back to a few other people within the organisation and get back in touch.

Now the key to this story is, I thought this was just a chat, not a job interview because I hadn't even applied for one. I was just happy to be sharing some of my thoughts and seeing where it would take me.

A couple of days later I got an email from the caller. They thanked me for my time and said they'd be interested in hearing more of my ideas in person, so would I be free to fly over and visit them at their headquarters – they said they'd cover flights, transport and food. Now obviously I said I'd have to check my schedule and get back to them, but who am I to turn down a free trip overseas!

Two weeks later I received an e-ticket and details of when I'd be travelling. Upon my arrival at the airport I found I was flying business class (nice!), and when I got to where I was going, discovered I was going to be staying in a 5 star hotel (not a bad start). The next day I got the opportunity to meet some of the senior team within the company and have a series of brain storming meetings – even though I was still not really sure why I was there. But when I get a chance to meet new people, it's always been in my nature to look at it as an opportunity, so I was happy with the way things went. At the end of the day, as the meetings drew to a close, the person I'd originally spoken to asked me if I'd be interested in taking a position with the company. They'd created a new role within the organisation for a Director of Global Digital Marketing. Just because of what I'd been talking about. I was stunned.

Now think back to earlier – I'd neither submitted an application nor applied for a job, yet a global brand had sought me out online solely on the basis of liking how I was using digital marketing platforms to increase awareness of a business, engage with customers and build what I like to call 'valued connects'.

My story reinforces the fact that many recruiters are now using social media and LinkedIn specifically to source talent for companies.

When I speak in schools and colleges, students love hearing this story. Many of them comment on how this example of using the Internet's tools positively can impact on their future. The number one question I get is 'Did I take the Job?' The answer is... 'No'. I am, always have been and probably always will be an entrepreneur and what I 'jokingly' call 'unemployable'. I was flattered, obviously, but I love what I do. (Though it might have paid better...) Who knows, the next opportunity like this for you could be just around the corner. So have a think – is the content you've created in the past, or are currently creating, going to help get you those opportunities? If not, why not!

Nowadays, everyone who's looking for a job or applying for college or university will have to engage with some sort of online process – making us all Digital Job Seekers. More and more companies are advertising jobs on platforms such as LinkedIn, so in order to make the most of career opportunities, we naturally have to start protecting our Online Reputation.

With this switch from traditional job seeker to Digital Job Seeker, one of the main differences will be how you make sure you stand out from your competitors. Finding innovative ways is key; luckily the Internet provides plenty of solutions when it comes to this. Research carried out by Workfolio found that '56% of all hiring managers are more impressed by a candidate's own website than any other personal branding tool – however only 7% of job seekers actually have a personal website'. So to get into the top 10% of job seekers who have the best chance of impressing nearly 60% of hirers – you know what to do.

/CREATING YOUR PERSONAL WEBSITE

Now, setting up a personal website these days is relatively straight forward. There are a number of free providers on the web - WordPress, eBlogger and Weebly are three which spring to mind. All of these platforms offer FREE templates you can use for your website and it's pretty much just a case of registering and adding your text - no super HTML or development skills needed. Yaaay!

Having your own personal website will not only help add more content about you for the search engines to find, but it gives you a space to update what's going on in your life on a regular basis – what you're getting up to, your thoughts on topics which might be of interest to other people... and your next employer. All of which help contribute to your digital portfolio.

Once you've got your Website up and running, remember to keep it updated. Many users simply forget about theirs – so adding regular content on a monthly basis or even more frequently is also a good way to stay ahead of the pack.

/WAYNE'S TOP TIPS OF WHAT TO INCLUDE ON A GREAT PERSONAL WEBSITE

1. Headline – something which sums up what you're about
2. Brief Bio – your 'about me' page
3. Resume – perhaps a shortened version of your CV or a link to download a PDF of the full version
4. Samples of your work – maybe a portfolio page which showcases some of the projects you've been involved in
5. Blog - this can show your personal development, areas you are interested in and articles you've written.

/LOOKS AREN'T EVERYTHING...
OH HANG ON, YES THEY ARE - IF YOU'RE A WEBSITE

One thing to remember when setting up your own Personal Website is that it needs to look good. Choose a theme which represents you and what you're about. Remember that potential employers will be looking at it, so it needs to function correctly, have a professional look and feel and, most of all, contain content which your next employer is going to appreciate.

As more and more people are going to be accessing your website from mobile devices such as smartphones or tablets, it's really important that you make sure your website offers a mobile responsive design. 'You what?' I hear you gasp. Don't despair. The good news is that many online providers, like Wordpress, have themes which are already fully mobile responsive. Which means you don't have to worry. When you're looking for a freebie template, or a paid one, remember to make sure it offers a mobile responsive version. If you've ever tried to access info from a non responsive website on your mobile, you'll know what I mean.

/INFOGRAPHIC CV

Many digital job seekers have started to get creative with the bog-standard CVs – which, let's face it, are traditionally pretty flat and boring (I know mine was!) The trend of Infographic CVs, started out by graphic designers, has now become an important tool in the Digital Job Seeker's toolbox. Now I expect you're wondering, 'What is an Infographic CV and how will having one help me land a job in this digital age?' Well, if you think back to my boring old typed CV, an Infographic CV is designed, so it's full of life and very visual. Let me explain...

The main purpose of an infographic is to compile large amounts of information and present it in an appealing, engaging and visual way to make it easy and interesting for the reader to understand and absorb. In a nutshell that's it.

Now you're probably thinking to yourself, 'Wayne I'm no Graphic Designer, so how am I possibly going to produce a brilliant Infographic CV with my limited/non-existent knowledge of Photoshop?' As ever, don't fret. All is not lost. You don't have to - but if you're a dab hand with Photoshop crack right on! For those of us, me included, with limited experience in design, there are now a whole bunch of online sites which can help solve this problem. Or, to keep up with this growing trend, just send off your LinkedIn profile info to a real-life, grown up Designer who'll populate the Infographic for you. Now do you see why having a LinkedIn is useful?

/INFOGRAPHIC GUYS

Here are some of the services specialising in the creation of brilliant Infographic CVs for you. Most are usually based on your LinkedIn profile using pre-designed templates:

- » visualize.me
- » re.vu
- » resumup.com
- » cvgram.me
- » coolinfographics.com

/THE VIRTUAL INTERVIEW

It's true! There is such a thing. In fact, virtual job fairs are becoming more and more common, especially around areas such as IT and Marketing where professionals are in high demand and headhunted globally.

Traditionally a job fair would have been an expo type event where you got the chance to wander around different employer stands, see who was recruiting and find out more information about them and the types of roles they had on offer. Many companies, if they needed to hire fast, would allow you to apply at the event and even attend an interview with a hiring manager on the same day.

With virtual job fairs – as the name suggests – you don't need to go anywhere. You just receive an invite to attend and you login from your computer, tablet or phone. Pretty cool right?

Once you get access, you can view the job fair, find out what companies are taking part, look at the jobs they have on offer, take any skills tests needed for interview and even participate in a live interview via the website.

The concept of virtual interviews is one which will continue to develop and will probably become a core component of the recruitment process. With this in mind, you can see how important it is to think about your Online Reputation and to have a good idea about what content is online about you. It only takes a potential employer a few moments to do a quick search on Google (while you're taking part in a virtual interview) to find out any information about you - be it positive or negative. Think about it!

/ALTERNATIVELY... HOW TO SCUPPER YOUR CHANCES OF GETTING A GREAT JOB

"It's difficult for a recruiter to 'unsee' these references."
Susan Vitale, Chief Marketing Officer at iCIMS, a talent acquisition company.

IN SHORT...

- » Incoherent shentenczs (drunk or sober).
- » Rambling on and on and on... sorry. Lost the will to live.
- » Mis-spellink. Spellcheck anyone?
- » CAPS LOCK ON FULL PELT
  (a favourite of my Mum's) - STOP SHOUTING!!!
- » Txtg Shrtctz – think someone will take the trouble to interpret what you're saying? Nah, too busy.

/WHO CAN VIEW AND WHO HAS ACCESS TO MY DATA

If your Social Media profiles are public, then a potential employer may have access to more information than just your qualifications and experience. Unless you think about and make regular changes to your privacy settings according to what information you want to share, there's probably a very good chance that information is being accessed about you right now (please close this book, check and then continue reading).

You're back? Good.

Now please don't think of checking your privacy settings as a simple one-off exercise. Many of our favourite social media platforms and smartphone apps change their privacy settings on a regular basis, so it's important you pay attention when you get the updates, and take notice of how the changes will affect the privacy of any of the content you've posted – as well as who has access to it. And remember to check all devices, changing your facebook settings on your laptop/ipad will not automatically transfer to your phone. You'll need to check it too.

/EVALUATING YOUR SOCIAL MEDIA

When it comes to Social Media, many of us never really ask the question 'Why are we using it?' Nor do we evaluate the platforms we're using and consider if they're still right for us or not. Think about this – are your old Bebo or MySpace profiles still kicking about? See what I mean? When the latest social media platform starts to get hot, many of us just move across with little thought about the places we were previously on and what information may still be lurking about on them.

One thing we can be sure of is that there'll always be new platforms popping up and if our friends join them, we probably will too. But what about those older platforms we've moved on from? Should we close those down and remove any information we don't want surfacing again, or just leave them dormant in the hope that Bebo might just make a comeback. (You may

TOP TIP
Remember to check out those older platforms we've moved on from. BEBO anyone?

laugh, but there is talk.) Whatever our reasons, evaluating our social media is important and it's something we need to carry out on a regular basis, and when platforms come and go.

/FOR SOCIAL MEDIA, READ LIFE!

It's a lot more than just evaluating our Social Media usage. We should really evaluate everything we do online – Social Media's only a small part of the Big Picture. We all need to get into the habit of looking at everything we post, share and upload online, and think about who can come across it, what it'll tell them about us and how we're living out our lives.

/USING PLATFORMS TO ENHANCE YOUR JOB HUNT OR CAREER

I recently got into a bit of debate with a colleague (also a lecturer) about a rather bold statement I had made about CVs becoming a thing of the past. My view was that we're wasting student's time encouraging them to spend time and effort putting a CV together. My point is – well I've touched on it already in the context of this book – that there's a massive shift in the whole recruitment industry, which has now gone online to find and source the best talent.

Social Media and the Internet provides the vehicle for employers to advertise positions and find talent. This is why LinkedIn has had such massive growth. Therefore I feel and, from what I have seen, I actively argue that spending time developing your Online Reputation, focusing on building your network and developing your LinkedIn profile will be far more effective in getting attention from potential employers and recruiters than a traditional CV, and is therefore much more likely to turn into interviews and job opportunities.

/TWITTER AS A GLOBAL AND LOCAL JOB BOARD

Everyone who knows me knows Twitter is my platform of choice. I love it. To date I've sent over 45.1k+ tweets. Some say I need to get out more. I tell them I tweet on the move 😊

NEWS. BREAKS. ON TWITTER.

Movers and Shakers 'Thought Lead' on Twitter. Twitter for me and many other people who use it effectively, is about far more than tweeting about what you had for lunch or finding out what celebs are doing to make themselves look less boring than they are. No names mentioned Gordie Shore People.

And now, many large recruitment agencies and also companies have begun to use Twitter as a way to advertise jobs – in 140 characters. These agencies and employers have found it to be an extremely useful method of reaching

I.LOVE.TWITTER.COM

job seekers in a more innovative and affordable way. Hashtags such as #Jobfairy have become an important way for potential job seekers to find new opportunities with companies.

Now you might just be scratching your head and wondering how could something with 140 characters help with my job search or get me a job.

Well grab a cuppa. Still awake? Let me explain...

As a potential job seeker, think back to what I mentioned earlier about creating and generating positive content and how it can help towards your job search. A really good start is to follow the Twitter accounts of companies which you'd love to work for. If you're following them, and maybe RT (retweeting) some of their content, well eventually they might just follow you back. (This is what you want People!) Once this happens, and if you're creating and sharing content which they find interesting, well, you might just be on their radar when they're hiring for the job you want... Sounds simple, right?

TOP TIP

Developing your Online Reputation will get you more attention than a traditional CV. Follow Twitter accounts of companies you would love to work for. Then impress them with your interest and informed comments.

/TOP TWITTER TIPS

(Try saying that after a couple of beers.)
In order to be successful, there are some things which you need to take on board to make Twitter work for you. Let me share:

» Have your own voice – you are unique, so be unique on Twitter. Find ways to create tweets which engage with your followers and reflect your own personality and interests. Whatever you do, don't just use it to follow celebrity gossip...

» Be authentic – your effort on Social Media needs to be 'real', it's key to not coming across as 'false'. Which is uncool.

» Follow the right people – Twitter has provided users with a unique way to connect with people which otherwise would have been impossible. It has provided responsible users with the opportunity to directly build and develop relationships with Thought Leaders and Influencers in their industry, as well as gaining valuable insight into how those leaders have become successful in their own right.

» Make your Profile stand out – this is the first thing people will see when choosing to follow you, and you only have 160 characters - so Make It Count.

TOP TIP
Invest in Yourself. It will be the best time/money you ever spent. Keep your knowledge up to date, relevant and current.

- » Engage with others – look for ways to follow and engage with others who really inspire you. Find ways to share their content and respond to their tweets.

- » Become a Thought Leader – why not! If you're passionate about something, start talking about it. Use Twitter as a way of getting your message out there, or perhaps pursuing a career path you want to get into.

- » Use of appropriate humour is always good - remember, I said appropriate!

When I started out, I watched how others were doing it. Not in a creepy, stalker outside your window sort of way, I hasten to add (well, at least, I didn't think so), but by observing their accounts, following them and retweeting stuff I found interesting. This helped me find my own voice when I started to join the conversations.

#Jobfairy is a useful hashtag to monitor when looking for job opportunities. Many companies will use this within their tweets for advertising job vacancies.

One of my mottoes in life has always been
/INVEST IN YOURSELF

The Internet, Social Media and particularly Twitter have lent themselves to that by helping me find experienced online professionals and Thought Leaders I could connect with and follow. And sometimes even find updates on programs they offer online that I could take advantage of – sometimes free and sometimes with a cost involved.

Because on Twitter I've developed an informed group of people who I follow and followers, I'm always able to keep up with the latest developments in my industry which helps me keep my knowledge up to date, relevant and current.

Now in order to get noticed on this platform it's important that you show What You Are Passionate About. Twitter is an excellent platform to let your personality shine. Building your network takes time, but it's something which can become very valuable. Potential employers and recruiters know this. With

Twitter, the best piece of advice I can give you, is don't get caught up in trying to build a large group of followers.
Numbers don't matter.

Focus instead on building a group of engaged, interested followers, regardless of how many there are. It's all about following the right people. And getting them to follow you.

Investing in Yourself can cost you financially or timewise, but you'll reap the rewards tenfold.

OK so I'm going to throw down the gauntlet to you my friend. Yes, you, not the person standing behind you!

I want you to think for a moment of 8-10 companies you'd love to work for. Think about how cool it would be if you could get a real working insight into those companies and perhaps connect with some of the people who work there... I can see you like that idea!

And here's the thing. With Twitter and other social media platforms it's possible. And by following people who work for the company you might get a much better idea about what it's really like to work for the company (compared to what you might see on the company's official Twitter account).

Another useful idea to help you get 'found' if you're looking for jobs via Twitter, is to use hashtags within your tweets. This will help recruiters narrow you down and give them greater potential to come across your tweet.

TOP TIP
Make your profile stand out. On Twitter you only have 160 characters. Drill down to what's great about you. On Linkedin it's 120. Make it count #BOOM

/LINKED IN - YOUR DIGITAL CV

Now you'll have heard me banging on earlier about Why I Think LinkedIn is One of, If Not THE Most Important Platform for Everyone With A Career... or thinking about a career, or between jobs or is a student prior to chasing a career.

LinkedIn has changed the game when it comes to the way employers source staff and recruiters find talent.

And let me tell you why. A quick search on LinkedIn from 18/3/2014 for the key word 'Marketing' in the advanced job search, returned results of 5,541 marketing jobs. Over 5,000 jobs at the click of a mouse! That's massive.

Just to be clear, platforms like LinkedIn are developing and more employers are using these platforms to advertise jobs and source talent. Therefore, for

you, the Job Seeker, the whole aspect of your Online Reputation becomes essential for new career opportunities.

The game has radically changed when it comes to job hunting and career opportunities. Our Parents would have looked in the local and national papers and gone to agencies and Job Centres seeking work. We now look online, and because of that, what we say and do in our Brave New Virtual World becomes of vital importance. To hear more on the future of job-seeking google 'Knowmad Society, Moravec et al' Time will be well spent.

/THE DOS AND SOME OF THE DON'TS OF LINKEDIN

Like Twitter, when it comes to using LinkedIn as a tool for job searching, there are steps you need to follow which will not only improve your chances of getting an interview, but will improve your visibility within the LinkedIn network and get you found easier.

/NOTE TO SELFIE:
FACEBOOK IS FOR SOCIALISING. LINKEDIN IS NOT.

This might seem like a simple bit of advice, but many people get it wrong and mix up what they post on Facebook on LinkedIn. Like Facebook, you can share on LinkedIn, but both platforms are polar opposites when it comes to how they should be used.

AVOID AT ALL COSTS linking your Facebook or Twitter accounts to LinkedIn – unless you want the hiring manager for that dream job viewing your pics from Saturday Night Out status updates – well, do you?

As of July 2015, LinkedIn boasted 380 million users world-wide – making it one of the most popular professional network websites in the world. If you like statistics, you'll love this – apparently LinkedIn gains two new users every second. That's popular!

But before you get stuck into setting up your profile on LinkedIn, spend a little time thinking about the type of career you're hoping to get in to. Once you have this clear in your mind, it'll help you develop your profile accordingly. Thinking about how you can build it with an employer in mind will also help you stand a better chance of connecting with people within your career choice, i.e. the people who matter.

Another thing to remember before you set up your career account is your email address – the one you want to be associated with your account. This is a step which many people just don't think about. You have to remember that potential employers will contact you via email, so perhaps having an address like hotbloke1999@yourmaleprovider might not be the best way to start off connecting with a potential employer. Unless your potential employer is a Kissogram Service. In which case that's probably OK.

So my advice, for the purposes of keeping things professional, is that it might be a good idea to set up a new email with a more appropriate address (just saying). Now, with those housekeeping rules out of the way, let's look at what goes into making a great LinkedIn profile - one that will Get You Noticed.

WHAT WE ARE GOING TO COVER HERE IS AS RELEVANT TO STUDENTS AND GRADUATES AS IT IS TO ANYONE SEEKING THEIR NEXT JOB MOVE:

» Attach a Profile Picture – it's essential to have a recent image associated with your LinkedIn Profile of you looking like a professional.

TOP TIP
Having an address like hotbloke1999@yourmaleprovider might not be the best way to start off connecting with a potential employer. Keep your email address professional.

» Most of the profile pictures are in colour, but I came across some recently who had black and white images which I thought looked cool — perhaps a way of standing out? Avoid a 'stuffy' or 'posed' look. Just a pic of you looking relaxed and 'normal'. And no bikini selfies puh-lease.

» Have a Headline, which packs a punch — a bit like Twitter, LinkedIn gives you the opportunity to create a headline consisting of 120 characters on your profile — The 120 Character Hook. This needs to include the most important keywords, i.e. what you're about. Think of it as your Evaluator Pitch for potential employers and make sure it packs a punch. #Boom!

» Have a Clear Call to Action — I don't want to start dropping the marketing jargon here, but within your profile you need to have CLEAR MESSAGING about Why You are The Type of Employee an Organisation Would Want to Hire. Have clear call to actions throughout the profile (and maybe some hyperlinks) which invite the person viewing your profile to find out more information about you. This helps in the process of getting them to contact you via email - or better still request a meeting or coffee.

» Your Summary is KEY- this is your Prime Real Estate and requires a well thought out approach. I've always found it best to sum up here what it is you're about, your qualities and experience. It's also the best time to hit them with notable clients or organisations you've worked with. Be careful you don't get carried away and make it all about how wonderful you are. Keep it concise. Remember the employer/recruiter BS radar will be up.

» Update all sections of your Profile – a poorly filled out LinkedIn profile is a bad thing. In fact you're probably better off not having one if you've not paid attention to detail when it comes to filling in the key areas of your profile. If you're a student, you may not be able to fill it all out, but at least covering the main bases will stand in your favour. Think about removing areas which are not relevant to you. As your career develops, make sure you regularly revisit your user account and update it.

» Recommendations are vital – our Parents know these as references. When you left one job, someone key within the company gave you a reference which you could use to say how great you are, for applying for future jobs. As with the traditional CV, the traditional reference format is also becoming a thing of the past. Many people now use LinkedIn as a place to display references which they've requested from other people, or companies. Having a good, rounded variety of references on LinkedIn is a great way to Boost Your Reputation on the network.

» Grow your network – as soon as you join LinkedIn, you'll find pretty quickly that you already have connections, i.e. people you know. Using the platform to start building your own personal LinkedIn network is a great way to increase your overall online/offline network. An important rule when trying to grow your connections is that if you are requesting a connection with someone, explain why you're asking. Don't just send them the default LinkedIn request as they might just delete it.

» Post regular updates — like on Twitter and Facebook, on LinkedIn you can post and share updates of what's happening in your professional career; or perhaps you've come across something you think connections in your network might be interested in, an event or an article maybe. Don't overdo it with the updates. You don't want to spam the place out as that would make your connections turn off. Think of ways where you can add value and share useful and interesting information. This helps you remain visible within your network and shows potential employers and recruiters that you are interested, informed and On Your Game.

» Join discussion groups - as of March 2013 there were 2.1 million groups on LinkedIn. Groups on LinkedIn are like discussion forums where users can chat about and discuss topics (who knew there were so many topics in the world!). Many recruiters use these groups to find the best talent who are actively engaged in them. Discussion groups are a great way for you to build up credibility and make new connections, so remember to ask questions - but also provide thought out answers.

/GETTING PROACTIVE NOT REACTIVE

When it comes to trying to find a job, it's better to be proactive and actively looking as this will seriously increase your chances of getting one. It's the same when it comes to your Online Reputation, being proactive is key to keeping it in check and in shape. It's about Starting Today. Many people make the big mistake of waiting till something happens, then act like a rabbit caught in headlights, frantically trying to create positive content all at once to counteract something negative which has appeared online.

As we mentioned earlier, there are many people online who can contribute towards your Online Reputation. Can you take a guess about any of them? While much of what is in this book so far focuses on the content which you create yourself and that which your friends might create and tag you in, there are others who can also contribute towards your Digital Tattoo, which you need to be aware of.

Think of your friends, family and co-workers who use the Internet and Social Media. These folks can contribute towards your Online Reputation in a positive way. And guess what? You get to return the favour. But for this to happen, they need to see that you're using the platforms in a responsible, positive way.

/ONLINE REPUTATION CASE STUDIES

PARIS BROWN

2013 was a year Paris Brown may not forget – nor indeed will the Internet. The 17 year old teenager was appointed as Britain's first Youth Police Commissioner with Kent Police – a job worth £15,000. But after only a week, she was forced to resign because of controversial tweets she'd posted on her Twitter account, aged just 14, which had been dug up by the Mail on Sunday newspaper, and published soon after her appointment.

On resigning, Paris commented that she had "fallen into the trap of behaving with bravado on social networking sites" and reflected that she hoped this would "stand as a learning experience for many other young people". Now this case has three interesting points. Firstly, it should act as a Wake Up Call to any of us 'who behaves with bravado', full in the knowledge that what we

say online can come back to haunt us. Secondly, that there are serious risks to your job and your career as a result of posting without thinking first, even if those posts were made at a young age. Thirdly, that her employer, Kent Police, did admit at the time that the vetting process did not normally require social networks "to be scrutinised for posts of this grade". But it didn't stop there. It later emerged that the tweets Paris sent were being investigated by Kent Police in connection to possible criminal offences after the force received complaints. Paris Brown now visits schools sharing her story.

/STUDENT ORDERED TO PAY $100,000 OVER TWITTER DEFAMATION OF TEACHER

I don't know about you, but in my book this is a Shed Load of Swag (if you are in the UK that's around £57,000). Perhaps a few year's wages for a Graduate just starting out. But this recent case, where a music teacher in Australia won a case against a former student who defamed her on social network websites Facebook and Twitter, has perhaps set things in context for many people. Or at least it should.

What's interesting about this case is that the person who carried out the defamation via social media, Andrew Farley, was never actually taught by the music teacher. It appears that he took a dislike to her because she replaced his father (also a music teacher) who stood down from the post in 2008 for health reasons.

The District Court Judge Michael Elkaim summed up that: "For some reason it seems that the defendant bears a grudge against the plaintiff, apparently based on a belief that she had something to do with his father leaving the school. There is absolutely no evidence to substantiate that belief."

The Judge went on to warn that "when defamatory publications are made on social media it is common knowledge that they spread; they are spread easily by the simple manipulation of mobile phones and computers. Their evil lies in the grapevine effect that stems from the use of this type of communication."

What happened here further highlights the fact that, as users of social media platforms, we need to be very careful of what we say online, because it may end up costing us a lot more than just our job. And we need to be aware of this very early on in life – like, say, Primary School.

Paris Brown and Andrew Farley learned this the hard way, and proved yet again legislation is finally catching up on online mis-use and that, as private individuals, we are subject to defamation law and other penalties and convictions for misbehaviour online.

JULIO REY WITH EVERYTHING AT HIS FEET... AND HIS FINGERS!

The transfer arrangements of Julio Rey (20) from Arosa FC fell apart, when his potential club Deportivo La Coruna, found a disparaging comment about the team that Rey had posted on his twitter account three years before, in 2012 aged just 17.

Harsh it might seem but Deportivo were understandably concerned with the account he was giving of his sportsmanship online. The club decided that his comments and his attitude did not reflect the character of their players and did not proceed with signing him. The Deportivo Club staff, like 93% of most employers and recruiters today display more than a passing interest in future employees' social media profiles.

This is just one of the numerous incidents of inappropriate or ill-judged social media postings among the footballing community. So many in fact that the FA are now issuing guidelines for players to reduce the risk of their reputation being damaged. Educating players to look after their reputation on social media is crucial as it not only affects them personally but also the reputation of the clubs, governing bodies - and of course multi-million pound transfer deals.

/BURGER KING FIRES EMPLOYEES FOR VIRAL PICTURE

A photo which surfaced on a website showing a Burger King Employee standing in two lettuce bins with the caption 'This is the lettuce you eat at Burger King' has cost not one, but three employees their jobs at the restaurant chain. The photo, which was taken as a joke, quickly went viral. 4Chan users (4Chan is a popular image based platform) were appalled at this fast food faux pas and it took them all of 15 minutes to track down the alleged perpetrator to his Burger King location, captioning the image 'This is the lettuce you eat at Burger King'. They had grabbed the GPS data enabling them to pinpoint exactly where the photo was taken resulting in Burger King firing 3 employees over the incident.

The thing to remember here (apart from never stand in lettuce in the workplace. Do it at home if you must) is, when you take a digital photograph using your smartphone, information is always attached to that picture. If you post that picture online, the information attached goes with it, so others have the ability to see the date and time that you took the picture, as well as where you took it – the GPS location is embedded.

/WE KNOW WHERE YOU ARE

It's somewhat scary and well worth remembering that when you upload a photo to Facebook, Twitter or anywhere online, people who view your images can use GeoTagging services on the Internet, Google Earth or Bing Maps to find out exactly where in the world the photo was taken.
You have been warned.

/PUBLIC SCHOOLBOY TWITTER TROLL

It seems when someone threatens to 'Tell our mother' it strikes a chord with the best of us. A prime example of this took place in 2013, when Internet Troll Oliver Rawlings used his Twitter account to make offensive sexual comments towards Cambridge University Professor Mary Beard. It all started when Oliver Rawlings (20) a student at Nottingham University (who'd previously attended the prestigious £10,344 a year Cheadle Hulme School) sent an offensive message in response to an appearance by the Professor on a BBC Radio programme.

But that was just the beginning, he continued with the abuse. Professor Beard decided not to take this lying down. She named and shamed Oliver, forwarded the attacking comments to her 42,000 followers – one of whom knew Oliver's mum. The woman kindly offered Mary Mrs Rawlings' home address in the wealthy gated-home area of Hale, Greater Manchester.

Oliver lost no time in backtracking with tweets of grovelling remorse. 'I sincerely apologise for my trolling', 'I was wrong and very rude', and 'Thanks 4 showing me the error of my ways'.

Too late. The press got hold of it and Oliver had to leave the country till the heat died down – 'recovering' from the backlash on his parents' yacht in Marbella. Poor mite. This unfortunately may not be an option in the fallout for most young internet mis-users. But they can always dream. On a positive note, 'Outing Your Troll' is now the name of the game which the braver Digital Citizens are playing – with some success, as the Mary Beard/Oliver Rawlings case demonstrated.

So. Just because we can doesn't mean it's a good idea. Many people who engage in trolling behaviour online seem to think it's acceptable to send hurtful and abusive messages to total strangers online. In the UK alone last year hundreds of Internet Trolls were prosecuted. The only trolls we want to hear about are ones in books who say "fol de roll". Agreed?

/TROLLS CAN GET JAIL SENTENCES. #FACT.

In 2012 in the UK, the Crown Prosecution Services reported more than 1,700 cases making it to court involving abuse sent online or by text message – up 10% on the previous year. A further 600 charges have already been brought against Internet and text bullies in the first five months of 2013.

/CELEBRITY CASE STUDY

Curtis Woodhouse, a former Birmingham City and Hull City football player and now a light-welter weight boxer offered fans and fellow tweeters £1000 to find the name and address of the guy who had been abusing him online for months. They obliged. Curtis decided to pay a visit to his troll's home and turned up at his doorstep after playing out the journey to amused fans on Twitter. Needless to say #keyboardwarrior 'Jimbob' did an Ollie Rawlings backtrack. Sorry Mr Curtis, I know I was in the wrong, it was just a joke blah blah. Google it.

/THE DIGITAL DILEMMA

The Internet has provided a whole host of new opportunities for us to communicate and share information with anyone at any time, anywhere in the world. I bet you can't remember the last time you sat down and wrote a letter to someone in a different country. It's actually more likely that you've never done this.

/CUE THE HOVIS AD MUSIC [GOOGLE IT!]

Eee, when I were a lad... I remember I had a pen friend in the States. When I was at School we used to sit and write letters, put them in envelopes, stick stamps on them and post them! If we were lucky, a few weeks later, we'd get a reply. Stop laughing at the oldies. It was the only way to keep in touch.

Emails have replaced the more traditional form of snail mail. And thank goodness! It's so much quicker just to draft something on your laptop, click Send and within a few moments the person you sent it to has received it,

hopefully read it and maybe even starting writing a reply. The ability to do this is actually pretty amazing.

With the development of Social Media and Smartphones, we've taken this to a whole new level. Now that we have Apps such as WhatsApp, we no longer need to sit down to even type an email. As long as we have WiFi or a data connection, we can send text messages anywhere in the world. And best of all it's FREE. Pretty amazing right?

Now let's look at it from another angle. Think of family members who have moved abroad in search of work in other countries. With the development of Facetime and Skype, we're able to have daily 'conversations' in real time via our webcams. Distance isn't such a big deal. In fact many businesses have been using this technology for years in the form of conference calls and video calls, which saves them the huge expenses of sending executives across the world for meetings. It truly is amazing.

/REAL WORLD V. VIRTUAL WORLD

But with us living in an ever-growing hyper-connected society, many of us are forgetting how to communicate in the 'real world' and how to build 'real' relationships compared to those in the 'virtual' world, which we've come to know and love.

Facebook's become a platform through which many people live out their lives, sharing absolutely everything which goes on within it. 'I'm off to the bathroom'. Yawn. Kidding, but you get what I mean. We've blurred the line between offline and online and for many people this is having an impact on their behaviour which, in turn, has a knock-on effect on their relationships with family, friends and work.

A study by the University of Michigan links social media usage with personality shifts and massive behavioural changes, both good and bad. It provided some very interesting insights which linked Facebook and Twitter usage with an increase in narcissistic personality traits in adults and students. According to the research in the study, students posting on Facebook are 'associated with the exhibitionism component' of narcissistic personality. Students posting on Twitter are 'associated with the superiority component of narcissistic personality'. The study further evidenced that those students posting on both Facebook and Twitter use the networks to show off while focusing on their appearances. Researchers discovered that the specific narcissistic trait exhibited depended on both the participant's age group and their preferred social media outlet.

What is Narcissistic Personality Behaviour (NPB) and how would I know if I have this going on? Hell, it goes without saying I must have it... but what about you? Well, NPB is defined as having 'an inflated sense of one's own self-worth'. Within the disorder there are several specific traits, including exhibitionism, superiority, entitlement, vanity, self-sufficiency, authority and taking advantage of others. We can see from this breakdown how social media would lend itself as a tool supporting these types of behaviour.

Researchers at Western Illinois University studied the Facebook habits of 294 students aged between 18 and 65. They established a direct link between the number of friends you have on Facebook and the degree to which you are a 'socially disruptive' narcissist. The research found people who scored highly on the Narcissistic Personality Inventory questionnaire had more friends on Facebook, tagged themselves more often and updated their newsfeeds more regularly.

This survey backs up other research which shows growing evidence that we, as social media users, are becoming increasingly narcissistic - obsessed with self-image and shallow friendships. Surely that can't be!

Carol Craig, social scientist and chief executive of the Centre for Confidence and Well-Being has said: "The way that children are being educated is focussing more and more on the importance of self esteem – on how you are seen in the eyes of others. This method of teaching has been imported from the US and is 'all about me'. Social media as public platforms are all about communicating with each other, mostly in 'the eyes of others', so keeping an eye on how we portray ourselves online and taking care not to 'embellish' or 'exaggerate' could help keep us running away with ourselves and letting our online selves get too 'swanky' as my granny used to say. Facebook provides a platform for people to self-promote by changing profile pictures and showing how many hundreds of friends you have. I know of some who have more than 1,000! Bet they're really close.

Now the question to ask is:

HOW MANY FRIENDS DO I HAVE ON FACEBOOK?

According to a study conducted by Arbitron and Edison Research, 18-24 year olds on Facebook boast an average of 510 Friends – that's a lot of people to keep in touch with.

Let's look at it from a different angle. To you what does the word 'friendship' mean? I suspect it's not the same thing as being friends on Facebook or any of the other social media platforms. Social media has, in some sense, diluted the meaning of the word 'friends', despite most of us being clearly aware of the differentiation. I suspect, like me, you have some people on your social media accounts that you, well maybe don't see from one month (or year) to the next. And could you call on these 'friends' in a moment of need? I thought as much...

/HAPPY BIRTHDAY TO ME...

Recently, one parent told me that her daughter had been really upset on the day of her birthday, not because of the number of cards they had received, or the gifts they received but because of the small number of 'Likes' on Facebook which they'd received from her friends. #QualityNotQuantity

/BECOMING A BETTER DIGITAL CITIZEN

Many schools are now starting to introduce into learning the concept of Digital Citizenship i.e. teaching young people how to become better digital citizens. Digital Citizenship is about creating safe, secure and ethical users of the Internet.

To become a Better Digital Citizen (BDC), there are a number of key areas to consider, which can help shape the internet for better and have a lasting impact on other users. Early pioneers of the Internet developed it with the idea of it being one global community. Many parts of the Internet are still like this, but others have changed as a result of developments on social media platforms. The Internet provides each and every one of us with great knowledge and great power. As the saying goes 'With Power Comes Responsibility' or as Spidey's Uncle Ben says, 'With great power comes great responsibility'. Great! As we all know, many of the platforms which we've come to know and love can also be used in hurtful and negative ways.

So, there are a number of things to think about in order to become a BDC. Remember social networking is still relatively young, just a teenager (probably like you), and still developing. So too are the guidelines in and around Digital Citizenship.

Don't forget that becoming a BDC is just as important for adults as it is for teenagers - so Adults reading this book Take Note – you too can be busted!

The number one thing to think about when it comes to using the Internet, Social Media or your Smartphone is to Think Before You Act. You've heard me say it before (just a few times Wayne):

STOP I THINK I POST

When it comes to things we say online and how we act, many of us still think there are no limits. This simply isn't true and sadly we've already seen examples of teens who've fallen on their sword when it came to their use of social media. They learnt the hard way. They didn't have the opportunity to read this book and put into action some of the suggested advice, which, if you use it, will be a Game Changer for your online and offline life, and that includes your career. So listen up - I'm going to run through some of the areas which I feel are very important for you to take on board to becoming a BDC.

Now I briefly mentioned earlier that Digital Citizenship is also important for Adults. Of course it is – it's the responsibility of our Parents and other important adults in our lives to help raise BDCs.

If you'd like some more info on digital citizenship, i.e. knowing how to behave appropriately when using the Internet, Social Media, Technology or your Smartphone, stay with me on this. Of course it's not just limited to the four areas I've just mentioned, but for the purpose of this book we'll focus on them.

/TO BECOME A BETTER DIGITAL CITIZEN

I've identified nine elements or themes, which make up digital citizenship:

1. **Digital Access** – it's hard to believe, but even in today's digital age we still have sectors of society where technology isn't available. Pick yourself up of the floor ☺. New technology has enabled many of us to develop new relationships, gain knowledge, create new communities and interact with each other in a fast paced environment. But not everyone has access to the same level and this is something which governments are working on, trying to create equality of access. Then again, there are some governments who are trying to hold back access to digital development. They know who they are.

2. **Digital Commerce** – the Internet has changed things for many of us, impacting on how we interact with retail brands, purchase products and even book our summer holidays, all as a result of digital commerce. But as good digital citizens, we need to be responsible and careful consumers when it comes to online purchasing. These days, we buy products very differently than our parents and grandparents did. It's important that we think about what we are purchasing, and the impact of buying. Think about how easy it is to buy something online – clicking Buy Now without even thinking about it – and as a result we can find ourselves in debt. This will affect our credit history, not to mention the stress of finding ourselves broke.

3. **Digital Communication** – is all about how we're communicating in a digital world. We've touched on this throughout the book as it's a core theme around Online Reputation. As a result of living in a hyper-connected society, most people who have a smartphone and data plan have access to a global audience in the form of a Facebook status update, Tweet or YouTube, amongst many others. But, and we've touched on this already, many users forget that this new form of communication can and may be saved for viewing later. Information will live on in 'cyberspace' long after we're gone. Morbid I know - but it's fact. It's really important that when it comes to the digital world, we understand what is acceptable and what is not. For the most part, the technology remains neutral, it's how we're using it, which causes most of the problems.

4. The technology, the platforms, the tools are changing all the time. This is all part of the digital age, which we all now live in, making Digital Literacy an important component of digital citizenship. Teaching in schools and the home is an important link in the process of developing good digital citizens for the future. Apple, I have found, have been proactive in the area of educating users on its products. When you buy a new MacBook, you can book a session in your nearest store to find out all the ins and outs of how to use the equipment. A great example of the teaching of digital literacy – but it needs to go further. Teachers in schools need to receive regular on-going training and support on how to use new technology, as well as the new and popular trends. This must also be transferred across to Parents to try to address the widening gap in knowledge.

5. Digital Etiquette – according to Ribble & Bailey (2007), digital etiquette is defined as 'the standards of conduct expected by other digital technology users'. When it comes to showing good examples of Social Media and the Internet being used as a Force for Good, we need more. Both the Internet and Social Media channels need more role models – or Champions for Change. In fact I believe the major social networks should be actively promoting users of this nature within the network, reaching out in order to showcase positive use. Digital etiquette is as important for adults as it is for teens. It's a set of principles which help make the Internet a better place for everyone. Digital etiquette is built around showing R.E.S.P.E.C.T. for each other online as well as using information appropriately. Students learn from other students and when it comes to technology, students watch how others are using it. Belatedly, we're only now beginning to develop rules and procedures for how technology should be used, and we still have so much more work to do. Negative digital use or mis-use can include inappropriate pictures, rude or nasty comments, or spreading gossip about others online. This of course extends beyond the Internet and social media to text messages too.

6. Digital Law – for a long time, the Internet was seen by many as a kind of virtual Wild West – with limited laws and powers to protect users. But over the past few years, this has started to change. Digital law looks very closely at the legal rights and restrictions governing the use of technology and questions are now being asked. Are people using technology the way it was intended or are they infringing the rights of others? The impact which file sharing has had, particularly in the entertainment industry, both in movies and music, demonstrates that many people today still don't think they're breaking any laws when file sharing music. Users need to better understand that issues on intellectual property rights and copyright protection are serious

and can result in severe consequences. But digital law now extends beyond intellectual property rights and copyright protection. Some users are now finding themselves in serious trouble for taking and sharing sexually explicit materials. An example of this is sharing nude or semi-nude pictures which has become quite common amongst users, in particular the whole aspect of 'sexting'. There are real dangers and consequences around this behaviour and if a participant is under 16 years of age, it can be considered child abuse imagery, even if the sender is a willing participant, and the sender – and others who have shared the image – can be arrested for the distribution of child abuse imagery. Many countries around the world have now passed digital laws and are working together across jurisdictions to bring people who engage in this sort of behaviour to justice. Laws for technology are developing and changing all the time to keep up with the rapid pace of technology.

7. Digital Rights and Responsibilities – think back to your first day in High School. Remember all the school rules and policies, and learning what was responsible and acceptable behaviour in class and school? Well, with digital use, also come rights and responsibilities. According to Ribble & Bailey (2007), Digital Rights and Responsibilities are the 'privileges and freedom extended to all digital technology users, and the behavioural expectations that come with them'. What this means is, as users of digital technologies, we must act responsibly and model appropriate behaviour in our digital society. Many of our schools and places of work have Responsible or Acceptable Use Policies (AUPs) on how technology should be used. As users, it's important that we stay within these to ensure everyone has a safe and positive user experience.

8. Digital Health and Wellness – according to Wikipedia, BlackBerry thumb is a new term that refers to a form of repetitive strain injury (RSI) caused by the frequent use of the thumbs to press buttons on PDAs, smartphones, or other mobile devices – yes this does happen, it's not a joke. When using computers, ipads, smartphones and other devices, our physical as well as mental health and well being is something which needs to be considered. Outside of psychological issues caused by Cyber-Bullying, Trolling or Stalking is Internet or Social Media addiction. Some experts are finding that withdrawal symptoms associated with Internet addiction are similar to those of alcoholics. We also need to consider issues such as hearing loss, back trouble or eye strain, all of which can present serious concerns if users are not encouraged to think about their own health whilst using technology. As how we communicate now is so immersed in social media and technology, and we play out our lives online, our mental health can be seriously affected by what goes on in our lives online whether that's positive or not so good.

9. Digital Security – I recently read a blog post about someone who had their identity stolen online and the battle they had to get it back. Many of us have gotten to a point where we freely share far too much information about our personal lives in public spaces online – yes on social networks. In the Interwebs there are Hackers and there are Snoopers. People who are actively looking for user information to use in a fraudulent way. As users of the Internet, it's important that we put systems in place, not only to protect ourselves, but also protect our information. You wouldn't go to bed at night without locking your front door and setting your home security system. Yet

for many of us, when it comes to our information floating about in Cyberspace, we leave it wide open! You need to keep your equipment up to date with firewall and anti-viruses which are your first line of defence. But also regularly updating and changing passwords is essential. Failing to protect your identity online can result in you falling victim to online scammers.

To not think about these nine elements as something which may or may not affect you is crazy. We all have a responsibility to keep ourselves, our friends and family as safe online as we would offline, and having the right information is a key aspect of doing it.

The Internet is still very young and, as a result, is evolving all the time. It's essential that you keep up to date on changes in these elements of Digital Citizenship and you look out for other users online. Reporting any suspicious behaviour, emails or links to platforms and services providers is always a good idea. It's your contribution to helping make the Internet a better place.

/THE WHAT'S WHAT GUIDE TO APPS

It seems like not a week goes by without some new app or Social Media website being launched, but you know what – it's absolutely true! By the time this book is published the market will most likely be flooded by hundreds more new apps.

Here's a quick overview on some of the Apps and Social Platforms which are currently in use, what they offer and what you might need to be aware of in order to keep your Online Reputation in check.

Now here's a scary thought – according to Cisco's 2012 analysis of global mobile data traffic * there are more mobiles than humans. I know. Crazeeeee! In fact many of us are carrying around two or three connected devices. (Well at least I do.)

Wow. That's impressive Wayne – but we're not all as geeky as you. Enough said. So here is my run down on What's Out There and what you need to be aware of. Remember each of these platforms and apps present many positive ways to be used but some of them, if not all present many risks too.

ASK.FM

Is effectively a Q & A website. It's a social network platform where users can invite questions from others via the site or from anonymous users. As of July 2014, it had over 65 million members and was hugely popular amongst teenagers. Users must be 13 to join and use the website.

TWITTER

A micro-blogging platform. Globally Twitter is estimated to have over 500 million users. Similar to a text message, users craft 'Tweets' which can have no more than 140 Characters. Users share pictures and videos and follow others on the platform. Users must be Over 13.

FACEBOOK

Facebook use is prolific amongst children and young people although many are now moving to, or also use, other platforms. It's also very popular with women over 55 so your granny may be on it. Facebook allows users to posts images, videos, comments, music, play games, share with friends and even purchase items, with many businesses now offering Facebook commerce. Users must be 13 or over.

INSTAGRAM

Instagram is used via a phone app allowing users to take pictures which can then be adjusted by applying filters. Images can then be shared on to Facebook and Twitter from the Instagram app. Users must be 13 to use the platform.

SNAPCHAT

Is a photo messaging mobile app is available for iOS and Android OS. As of February 2014, it had 100 million Unique Users posting over 400 million snaps per daily. Users can take pictures, record video, add text and drawings – known as 'Snaps' – and send them to a controlled list of recipients. Users can choose how long the image is to be available for up to a maximum of 10 seconds, after which it will be deleted from the receiver's device and from Snapchat. Snapchat states that 'Minors aged 13-17 should have permission from a parent or legal guardian before using Snapchat'.

SNAPKIDZ

Users under 13 who sign up for Snapchat are given access to Snapkidz. It works by allowing users the facility to take images and videos, add captions and drawings and save them on their mobile device. They are not shareable. At the moment.

SNAPHACK

Just launched in 2014, Snaphack allows you to save photos and videos sent through Snapchat without informing the person/s who sent them! We've even heard that an updated version of Snaphack has already been submitted to Apple – this version allows Snapchat recipients to share the saved images with friends on facebook and twitter.

VINE

Is a mobile app, owned by Twitter, which allows users the facility to create, post and share video clips of up to 6 seconds. Vine is currently available for iOS, Android and Windows Phone 8 OS. Users must be 13 to use the platform.

VINEKIDS

According to the good folks from Vine, a colleague was talking about how much his two-year-old daughter loves Vine - he said he wished there was a separate app so she could watch posts that are appropriate for kids. Naturally, one of the key differences in the new Vine Kids app is that the content is appropriate for children. Once launched the App serves up a mixture of content which most adults would find a little annoying but which kids would love. I came across one of Elmo, a pug dog saying "I love you" and interestingly enough, a hedgehog playing the piano – kids will love watching their favourites a few million times. Will make a change from Frozen then.

WHATSAPP

Popular cross platform instant messaging app for smartphones. WhatsApp is particularly popular with teenagers and has over 419 million active users – with 325 million photos shared every day. According to WhatsApp's terms, service users must be 16 to use it. The app is currently free for the first year. Facebook recently purchased this for a whopping $19bn (£11.4bn) - pretty amazing!

FOURSQUARE

Is a location-based app which allows users to check in at, for example, a local coffee shop or cinema. Once the users 'check-in' they can post a message about the place or take a picture and share it to Facebook and Twitter. Foursquare has over 30 million users with over 3 billion check-ins. Users must be 13 years of age to use the platform.

TUMBLR

This is a micro-blogging and social networking platform which allows users to post multimedia and other content to a short form blog. Users of Tumblr can post texts, photos, audio and video. In July 2014, Tumblr boasted 192.9 million blogs with 83.1 billion posts. Users must be 13 years of age to use the platform.

SOCIALCAM

A smartphone application which enables users to create videos and share them with friends. It's currently available on iOS and most Android devices. Similar to Instagram, once a user creates a video, they can apply filters, themes and soundtrack. Users can tag people in videos and share what they've created on Facebook, Twitter or YouTube. Users must be 13 years of age and under parental supervision until 18 years of age.

PINTEREST

An image and photo-sharing platform which allows users to create pin boards based on events, interests and hobbies. Pinterest users can search and browse other boards and 're-pin' images to their own board or Like things which they have found. Users can follow other's boards if they have similar tastes in art, travel, food, film, and humour. Most of the site's user-base is female. Pinterest offers a web-based platform as well as an iOS app. Users must be 13 years of age.

VIBER

Similar to WhatsApp, Viber is a smartphone application which offers users free calls, texts and picture sharing. Users can make free HD quality calls to other Viber users on iPhone, Android, Windows phone, Blackberry over 3G/4G or WiFi connections. Viber has over 200 million users. According to its privacy policy, Viber 'is not intended for or designed to attract anyone under the age of 13'.

SKYPE

One of the earlier pioneers in the voice-over IP service. Skype allows users to communicate with other users by voice using a microphone, video or by using a webcam and instant messaging over the Internet. Users can look up other users via Skype and add them to a contacts list. Users can also share video, images and files via the platform.

TELEGRAM

An App which allows users to send messages to other users similar to WhatsApp but with the added feature of your messages being sent as 'Secret Chats' - messages which can be sent with end-to-end encryption leaving no trace on the company's servers, and letting you set self-destruct timers on messages. Telegram has developed further enhanced security that allows you check the security of your Secret Chats using an image that serves as an encryption key. By comparing your encryption key to a friend's, you can effectively verify that your conversation is secure.

CONFIDE

Once downloaded, this app allows users to create and send messages which, when viewed, disappear. It has a User Interface (UI) which offers 'Screenshot' protection; this alerts users if a recipient has attempted to take a screen shot and offers them "End-to-end encryption, which is an uninterrupted protection of the confidentiality and integrity of, transmitted data by encoding it at its starting point and decoding it at its destination". Enough of the techno-jargon thanks Wikipedia. With the Confide app, text is blocked out and can be seen only when you slide your finger over the screen. According to Confide their app enables you to 'Say what you want, honest and unfiltered'. The website encourages you to 'Go off the record with self destructing messaging'. Messages disappear after they're read, ensuring all of your communication remains private, confidential and always 'off the record'.

POPCORN CHAT

Popcorn Chat messaging allows you to chat privately with other users in a one mile radius of your smartphone. The idea behind the app, according to the description on iTunes, is to 'immediately discover what people around you are doing – converse with others at live events, meet new people, and share meaningful thoughts amongst the local community'. Popcorn goes on to rave about its suitability for 'school campuses and dorms, concerts and conventions, visiting new cities, or just getting through a boring day at the office'. Bet your Boss (and Parents/Teachers and anyone who works with kids) will be happy to hear this. Just so we're clear, it also encourages children in its iTunes description to use it to 'Chat at school when you are bored in class'.

BEETALK

Another smartphone app which offers similar features to some of the others. Beetalk allows users to chat in what it calls 'Whisper' mode, allowing you to send messages which, after they've been read, disappear. With the BeeTalk app users can have access to unlimited calls and messages and set up group chats. The app also offers users the ability to send stickers and doodles to other users in your contacts list. If you shake the phone it will use your location-based services to find people who are near you, allowing you to view their profile and chat with them.

KIK MESSENGER

Another free app which has been growing in popularity with Teenagers. Kik Messenger allows users to text friends who are also using the app. One of the reasons it has become popular is that it allows users to do much more than just sent a text message, as users can add videos and images too.

CLOAK

Once it's connected to your Foursquare and Instagram accounts, this app allows you to see where all of your friends are, based on the location-based services. The idea behind it is if you want to avoid someone, the app will show you where they're located on a map – users can tweak settings to determine what kind of distance you want to keep from people, for example half a mile.

SHOTS OF ME

It seems even Justin Bieber is getting into the smartphone app business by financially backing the Shots of Me app. The app allows users to take selfies, share them with its 'selfies community', and also share them on via Twitter or Tumblr. Users of the app can also 'like' other people's selfies and tweet a link to them or share them on Instagram.

FLING

Fling allows you to 'fling' texts, pictures or video messages out to cyberspace to random receivers. Up to 50 users, in any part of the world can receive your 'flings'. The general location of your far flung messages are plotted on a map you can view. Unlike Snapchat, 'flings' don't seem to have a time limit – you are free to revisit these at any time. So sending something which might come back to haunt you at a later date is a possibility. Users should be 13+.

FACEBOOK ROOMS

Just launched, Facebook's anonymous based app allows users to create anonymous based chat rooms. A 'Room' is a feed of photos, videos and text with a topic determined by whoever created the 'Room'. Rooms can be shared through invitations which look like QR Codes. Same rules as Facebook apply in terms of signup. There is no check on age for users of 18+ Rooms.

CALCULATOR%

The App 'Calculator%' does exactly what it says on the tin . . . and then some! It looks and functions like a normal calculator with all the features you would expect. The bombshell is that it also allows users to hide images they're sending and receiving in a secure vault.

In order for the secret vault to function, the app needs permission to access the users' photos and camera. This allows the user to move across any pictures from their phone into the secret vault, which will be passcode protected upon download. Look out for the slight variation in the App's tile to distinguish between it and a traditional calculator – parents you need to make sure everything adds up!

AIRDROP

AirDrop is set up to use Wifi and Bluetooth to share files between a sender and recipient that are no more than 10 metres apart from each other.   If you have AirDrop enabled, you are able to receive files/messages/images from senders within a 10 meter radius. Users do have the option to reject a file that's being shared with them, but it still shows an uncensored preview of the image that's being sent.

So you can share videos, photos, websites, locations etc to other people with an iPhone within a 10 metre radius. However, some have more sinister uses for this App, using it for 'cyber flashing'. While the term is probably self-explanatory I'll explain anyway, it's the sending of an unsolicited indecent image via the Apple Air Drop feature to someone in close proximity.

While I hope these incidents don't become frequent, remember:
1. Turn the Air Drop feature to 'Off' or 'Contacts Only'.
2. Don't accept files from strangers over Air Drop.
3. AirDrop is specific to IOS and apple devices so parents of android users can breathe a sigh of relief . . .

BLAB

Blab.im is an exciting new video chat app, taking things to a whole new level. It allows up to 4 people to video chat simultaneously, allowing others to watch and comment on the stream. Of the four who are in the video stream, they can drop out at any time, allowing another viewer the opportunity to join the video stream.

To sign up to Blab video messaging app all you need are you Twitter login details followed by prompted easy steps. It's certainly one live video streaming platform to keep an eye on.

LIVE TEXT FOR YAHOO

With the tagline 'quick, personal, kind of fun'. Let's take a look at just what LiveText is all about.

The app is also ephemeral, (of course) deleting your chats and video as soon as the app is closed. While it might seem just a little strange to be using a Live Video App without sound this seems to be the USP with this new messaging app – users can exchange live video, text and emoticons – without any audio. Yup my friend it's silent. For those who love video and texting but not up for a chat – this is for you!

JOTT

Jott is an App that allows you to message without a data plan! It works by using a 'mesh network' operating on Bluetooth or using a router that can span 100 feet of users, using the trademarked 'Airchat' feature.

Similar to Snapchat – Jott also offers disappearing messages and screenshot detection. It's easy to see how the Jott App might just catch as other Apps such as Kik or WhatsApp requiring a dataplan or at least wifi to function. Jott App is certainly filling the void for those younger teens to be able to text. With Jott teens also don't need to know each other's numbers – those at the same schools can just look each other up via the closed system and start to chat. Allgood calls the app 'the equivalent to passing notes in class for the digital era'.

BURNBOOK

Burnbook has hit the headlines recently in the US, where parents and teachers are expressing outrage over this new anonymous social networking app, accusing it of being designed to encourage cyber bullying and is bringing 'threats of violence to their schools' (Mashable).

Basically once you have installed the app you can search for 'communities', ie schools near your location. Once you have found a community and join, you can then post anything, on any topic, within the community. According to Burnbook these can be anything from 'jokes, fails, wins, sightings, shout outs, revelations, proclamations and confessions — they all happen on Burnbook. Together, we can keep a secret'. The inspiration for the App's name is unsurprisingly from the movie titled 'Mean Girls' - need we say anymore?

At the moment at least Burnbook is Stateside – but that's not to say it won't extend its' reach to the UK or Ireland quite soon with the huge growth in popularity amongst teens for new anonymous apps to communicate with. Note to teachers and parents – Yet again, evidence that being aware of new apps, how they might be used and their risks and benefits has to be a duty of care.

WIPER

App-tly named (see what I did there?) as it literally 'wipes' messages from the sender's phone, recipient's phone and the company's own servers in seconds! This app appeals because it offers privacy and control over your data. In additional Wiper Messenger uses automatic end-to-end encryption for messages and calls. Users are alerted if their conversation partner screenshots the conversation. Users can also enable passcode protection for the app, offering another layer of protection to local users of the Wiper App.

SOBRR

This is one of the latest ephemeral apps, which promises users that the content, they call 'moments' will be erased in 24 hours. Yip you heard it right. 24 hours. Despite its name and the concept's birth being a result of a Hangover Stylee Stag night in Vegas; according to the apps founder Bruce Yang, this is not an app for when you're drinking. Heaven Forbid. That might be seen as socially irresponsible!

Once you have the app up and running, if you snap a photo which is called 'Vibing' and post it on Sobrr, people in your geographical can view the post. But just the once. They can then choose to cheer, comment or add you as a 24 hour friend. The term 'Friend' being slightly over-used nowadays. Just saying.

Now in order to get chatting to this '24-hour friend' you must accept their friend request and you can use the Sobrr Chat to have a conversation with them. As you can only have your new 'friend' for 24 hours, once the time has passed, you are cleared from each other's friend list, unless both sides opt into 'Keep'. Within the App you can also search for people nearby and choose to add them as a 'friend'.

According to the Sobrr website the App is all about 'creating a space where nothing is recorded, so you are free to share your life in the moment and meet new people without feeling restricted by your future self'. In short say and do what you want, on impulse, share it and dontworryaboutititsgonein24.

Kind of contradicts my STOP I THINK I POST approach.

MEERKAT, PERISCOPE & YOUNOW

The live streaming video apps Meerkat and Periscope give users the ability to broadcast live video directly to their Twitter followers. Watchers can view your video and re-stream to any of their followers in real time. Your own streams can be kept locally on your phone, but never on the cloud.

'YouNow' seems to be the preferred live streaming app of teen choice. On first inspection of the YouNow App it's very strange indeed – to us adults. As soon as you launch the App it starts streaming a live video of a teen singing in what looks like her bedroom – there were over 333 people watching the live stream, with viewers commenting below the video in a live chat.
YouNow shows how long the user has been broadcasting, typically this consists of users broadcasting from between 1.5 and 3 hours, singing, dancing or even sleeping. Yes. Sleeping. #Sleepingsquad is trending.

Live video streaming apps may be in their infancy but one thing's for sure, their popularity is growing and because Twitter is all about 'The Moment', all three of these apps seems to fill a void, at least for now, in allowing users to send out a link to their live broadcast video on what they are actually doing – right now.

#Overwhelm

Ok, take a deep breath and try not to panic. It's very easy to become overwhelmed by this wealth of information and the perpetual App development. Don't fret, it is my job to keep up to date and share this information with you! Just sign up for my newsletter or read the hints and tips on the blog or if you would rather watch than read, check out digital dilemma video series, **www.waynedenner.com/video** or podcasts on iTunes.

/CAUSE I'M APPY
[PHARRELL HAPPY TUNE DA DA DA...]

'85% of women and 72% of men aged 16-24 in the United Kingdom actively use social media apps on their mobile. Social networking finished in clear place... with 81% using these apps, ahead of games (70%) and music (56%).
(Voxburner, Young People and Apps July 2014)

So it'd be crazy not to use 'em for reach and engagement. Wouldn't it?

/FOR EXAMPLE

Apps like Snapchat get a bad press but again it's all about how it's used. I use Snapchat Stories extensively to get messaging out there. Check out waynedenner on Snapchat for updated Tips on keeping your Online Reputation in Shape. They're available for a 24 hour period, are really effective and all from the comfort of your Snapchat account. Clever eh? Snapchat continues to reign with Facebook and Twitter looking on in awe. Let's face it – it's everywhere.

In May 2014, according to Snapchat's figures, the app's users were sending 700 million photos and videos per day, while Snapchat Stories content was being viewed 500 million times per day – not bad for an App, which has only been kicking around since September 2011.

Many people, individuals and businesses in my opinion, are missing a massive trick in relation to how the app can be used and the benefits of it's Snapchat Stories feature. Now I've already blogged recently on how West Midlands Police have caught onto the whole idea of using Snapchat Stories to engage with their youth audience. As I mentioned I've begun recently to create my own Online Reputation Snapchat Stories using other platforms such as Twitter and Facebook to encourage users who are active on Snapchat to follow me.
 Each week I create a meaningful Snapchat story around the area of protecting your Online Reputation and managing your Digital Tattoo. This could be an image or a short video I share as a Snapchat Story- which will be available for

up to 24 hours on my feed.

I'm only testing the water but can see massive potential for others to jump on board with this approach, especially those looking to engage with a young, mobile savvy audience. This could be a massive opportunity for individuals, businesses and brands to use the channel as a creative way to engage with a whole new audience.

But and it's a big but, people tend to forget social media is about a 2-way conversation. It's not all about spamming up your audience with your business or personal messages. The content you create has to have meaning to them.

Snapchat usage is prolific with upwards of 80% of students in the schools I speak in now using the app regularly – beating Facebook, Twitter and Instagram. To see how I'm doing it search waynedenner on Snapchat.

/SO... IS YOUR HEAD SPINNING YET?

Your digital footprint is everywhere and it may stretch back further than you think. If you are an adult reading this book – and I'm glad you are – check back across your earlier days on the Internet and delete and deactivate older profiles. Perhaps you still have a MySpace profile kicking about (I did). Remember that? Profiles such as these could still be showing up in search results and not doing your Online Reputation any favours.

Conducting a regular Online Audit on yourself is always a good idea because of the nature of new content being created on a regular basis. The results within the search engines may change from time to time so it's always a good idea for you to be on top of this, and know what's out there before a potential employer or college recruiter comes across it.

If something negative is on the Internet, it's difficult to get it removed completely. The Internet does not as yet have a delete button and any mistakes we've made can be found easily online. Our best hope if something like this happens is to know about it and create more positive content on a regular basis in order to push the mistakes further down the search rankings.

While Google does offer a removal tool which can remove some content from search results, the process often takes some time. This can cause those concerned much distress and continue to damage their reputation. While progress has been made getting search engines to deal with content of a negative or defamatory nature, it still presents problems. Social networking platforms have also had the problem of users setting up fake accounts and posting negative and or defamatory comments about other users. While many platforms claim they have a robust process for dealing with cases like this, they still have more work to do in addressing such content more quickly to relieve undue distress on the person it's connected to.

On a lighter note, just for fun, there are some brilliant parady accounts out there.
Check out https://twitter.com/notzuckerberg and https://twitter.com/Queen_UK

/INTERNET NASTIES

Now if you're someone over the age of 21 reading this blog, you are forgiven, just this once, for thinking a troll is some sort of mythical creature living under a bridge. Sadly this is just not the case. Although there may indeed be some mythical folk online, trolling is an activity which is increasing rapidly in humans. And it's just not cool. In fact online trolling has serious effects – recent research reports that 1 in 3 young people aged 14-18 have received offensive online comments – and 1 in 10 have themselves trolled (Time to Change Report, 2014).

The survey also found that One in 3 young people have been the subject of trolling in the last six months, and and One in 4 are affected by it regularly.

Out of the 2,000 teenagers involved in the research, it was found that the majority of offensive online comments by 'trolls' are in respect to the victim's appearance (40%) or about their religion or race (16%). Facebook is the most common platform for victims to be trolled. And this behaviour is escalating! Come on Facebookers, there's just no need.

/I CANNOT STRESS THIS ENOUGH

What's most alarming is that so many individuals are getting enjoyment out of causing pain and hurt to others in this way. Many trolls do it because they think it's funny. It's not. It's thoughtless, cruel, harmful and can lead to some serious consequences such as depression, self-harm, and sometimes force those who've endured it for some time to contemplate or attempt suicide. A few even succeed.

Many people who use Social Networks such as Facebook and Twitter might be sick of hearing messages from me (if you haven't seen such messages, stop everything and follow me right now!) in relation to lifestyle skills, tips and awareness on how to use social media platforms towards a better internet and to your advantage. Encouraging young people not to troll and making them aware of the consequences of trolling is important.

Now with cases of Internet trolling on the rise it's important that you know how to deal with an online troll, so I've come up with Three Steps to help keep you safer online.

The first one is a really important one. I want you to remember it and spread the word. It could help dramatically reduce some of the negative experiences your friends and family encounter online...

- » NEVER, EVER, forward on a video, comment or message attacking someone else. Don't be tempted, no matter how 'funny' or 'interesting' you think it might be. Just to be clear, I use 'attacking' in the physical, verbal and, hell, basically any other/all contexts. If you remember this, you're halfway there already. Give yourself a Gold Star.

- » If you're trolled, Block the User. This should always be your first step. If someone's sending you messages which you feel are hurtful, unkind or inappropriate, then your best course of action is to block them. On my Twitter account, for example, I sometimes find a user who's followed me and is sending inappropriate messages which may be hurtful towards either myself or others. Without hesitation, I block them.

- » Keep a record of inappropriate or hurtful messages. Get familiar with how to Print Screen and make a folder. Keep details of the sender if possible.

/NEVER FEED THE TROLLS

This means winding someone up until they post trolling comments. It's just not tennis. Trolling is a dangerous game. You have no clue who's going to join in. And things can get out of hand. Don't get involved. You could create a monster. You know better than that. It's not big and it's not clever.

TOP TIP
Watch what you Snapchat. Third party apps can save and share without your knowledge. If you don't want it coming back to haunt you, don't send it.

/SOCIAL MEDIA &
THE LONG ARM OF THE LAW

Social Media platforms, particularly Twitter and Facebook, have for many businesses, organisations and public figures, become the all important communications tool as they're quick, free and have an unimaginable reach.

Northern Ireland has recently seen a high profile example of comments coming back to haunt us. And this time the posts aren't from children and young people, but 'mature' adults, some of them with media experience or holding a position in public office. They know who they are.

In 2013, a high profile Councillor was arrested and charged in connection to an investigation into 'the sending of grossly offensive communications and other serious criminal offences in relation to intimidation and encouraging criminal acts'. As charges were reviewed by the Public Prosecutions Service (PPS) in relation to comments about a proposed fictional 'massacre' at a (real) Nationalist March (try to keep up), the Councillor accepted responsibility and apologised for posting her views in the public domain. Her "lack of judgement" (her own words), again demonstrates the need for consideration before posting at all times, whether you're in public office or not. The Councillor received an official warning by the Police and was lucky not to have been prosecuted.

This and other recent events have again reinforced the fact that it's not just children and young people who can be impulsive, immature and thoughtless online. Sadly many adults, including those in positions of public office, are falling victim to the propensity to spew private views and thoughts into ill thought out (if thought out at all) public posts.

Provocative public speaking is nothing new. However in the digital age, public figures' Twitter posts and Facebook comments are scrutinised to within an inch of their lives, and even the most well thought out and carefully crafted posts can be found wanting by the public. The press is jammed with cases of individuals and companies getting into hot water over inappropriate or negative online use.

Twitter itself was in the spotlight because of its less than sensitive handling of the journalist and feminist Caroline Criado-Perez rape and death threats from Isabella Sorley and John Nimmo. Perez's tenacity highlighted the torrent of abuse directed towards women online which have previously been tolerated. Ms Perez told Twitter to 'get a grip' and police to 'step up' in their dealing of these now all too frequent incidents. Sorley and Nimmo were jailed, Twitter updated the service to include a Report Abuse button, and the UK boss was forced to apologise for not taking online abuse seriously in the past.

But this all serves to reinforce the message that inappropriate and negative use can have serious repercussions to your reputation, employment, standing in the community and in extreme cases can lead to arrest, convictions and maybe even some jail time. In the UK, you can look forward to 6 months in jail or a £5,000 fine under the Malicious Communications Act (1988) if convicted – and some MPs are calling for stiffer penalties.

Members of the public are also increasingly prepared to explore the legal options available to them if Social Media posts stray into areas of defamation, harassment and breach of privacy. So there you have it, a disgruntled Facebook 'friend' may now seek legal representation, rather than slugging it out online.

Many digital citizens, as well as the authorities, are no longer willing to ignore the Free-For-All the Internet has become. Significant efforts by individuals, governments and organisations are being made to tame the 'Wild West' web and there will be casualties. So take care out there cowboys.

I'm all for free speech but there's little tolerance for abuse, 'incitement' and misuse online out there now. And who's to say that's a bad thing. Isn't it time more emphasis was placed on making the internet a better place as well as a safer place? Exploring the potential of this amazing tool and what it can do for our life and career opportunities?

/THE FUTURE

Over the past few years we've seen technology pick up at a rapid pace. I can still remember my Commodore 64 ('Your what?') which played video games that were loaded up by a cassette tape, (c'mon you know what a cassette tape is). But back then, of course there was no Internet. As the saying goes, it was just one kid, his joystick and hours of gaming fun ☺.

The technology I 'was' using back then was a lot safer but it a LOT more basic than we have today. And it was a lot safer to access.

As I've gotten more involved in speaking to young people in schools and at events - I've spoken to thousands now, it's been no surprise to learn that the technology isn't the problem - it's how it's being used that is.

Creating awareness of how the internet can be used as a tool for creativity, general usefulness and to enhance and maximise life, learning and employability opportunities is the way forward.

You are the first generation of teens and adults in the digital age. Your children in the next generation will be even more more technologically savvy, but you're the guys with the unique opportunity to influence future use.

The Internet is a different place today than it was 10 years ago. Governments around the word have begun to focus on not just improving safety with major ISPs and Social Media Platform providers, but educating young people on how they can change their lives with technology.

This work needs to continue as we're starting to see an even younger user base beginning to access technology. Did you know that 38% of under two's have used a Tablet device (Ofcom: Children and Parents Media Use Report). Even for a buff like me, that seems just crazy. But that's the way it's going. 75% of children aged 8 and under have access to a 'smart' device. And they're using them.

Like it (excuse the pun) or loath it, Facebook is at the heart of a new 'Social Sign In' age. Many websites, email providers and even online stores now allow users to sign in with their Facebook login. This can only grow if continued advancements make the Internet a safer and more secure place to communicate, share information, build relationships, do business and connect globally.

As this new, technology driven world we now live in continues to expand, our Online Reputation will become paramount to how people perceive us. As users of Social Media and the Internet we need to realise that our Online Reputation will become an ever more integral part of who we are and how we are perceived. We can take control.

START TAKING CONTROL

WILL YOU MAKE SOCIAL MEDIA MISTAKES THAT WILL COME BACK TO HAUNT YOU?

OR HAVE AN EPIC ONLINE REPUTATION THAT WILL OPEN UP OPPORTUNITIES YOU ONLY DREAM OF?

MAKING GOOD CHOICES ONLINE IS KEY.

/SHAPING YOUR FUTURE REPUTATION

Last word from Wayne..

There's absolutely no doubt in my mind that Social Media, the Internet and technology will continue to develop and evolve. So too will the impact of your Online Reputation on your Life Choices.

Statistics like '93% of recruiters are using social media', '66% of recruiters are using Facebook' and 'one in every four recruiters has hired from Facebook' might have opened your eyes and made you go 'OMG!' – but it's a fact. 'Fair' or even ' legal' doesn't come into it. It's what's happening out there in the world of Jobs You Want.

According to Jobvites 2014 Social Recruiting Survey '83% of recruiters are turned off by posts on drug use, 70% by 'sexual posts' and 44% by alcohol related posts'.

Increasingly, we're going to see a lot more of this shift with employers using Social Media to screen applicants for potential job roles. And if you've been paying attention to what I've been banging on about in this book, you now know how important it is to be increasingly mindful of your Digital Tattoo and what it says about who you really are.

Digital platforms are moving as fast as an out-of-control train. But on the other hand, your Online Reputation is in your control. We can all control the content we post online. The stuff we post and share can, and does, have an impact on the opportunities we get.

In the future, we're going to see more of a focus on wearable technology. In fact it's already started. Social media platforms are already looking at ways to integrate wearable technology into platforms and it won't always be limited – as it currently is – to just receiving notifications.

Twitter was at the forefront with its micro blogging platform. Many scoffed, saying that sending something in 140 characters would never catch on. And indeed, many still don't get it (at least some people I come across... no names mentioned). But one thing is for sure – it's changed the way we get access to what's happening in the world. It's where news breaks.

We're entering a new phase - which is all about being connected in micro moments. For many of us our smartphone is always with us – an extension of our arm. Given that we're willing to carry them around at all times, think of how wearable technology will impact! Over the next 12-24 months we're going to see much more than just Google Glasses and Samsung watches. Although both are pretty cool (if either company wants to send me a freebie I'd be very appreciative [need a winking smiley here ;)].

Many new tech companies are already competing to be the next big thing in wearable technology and whoever's first off the blocks will likely get snapped up by one of the major social network providers. Word in Techie Land is already saying that 'wearable technology will become as indispensable as smartphones in the next three years'. According to some interesting research from Nielsen on today's consumers, '15% currently use wearable technology, 50% want to buy it and 70% know what it is'.

/BUT WHAT DOES ALL THIS REALLY MEAN FOR MY LITTLE OLD ONLINE REPUTATION AND ME?

In a nutshell, as users of the Internet and Social Media platforms, we're going to be creators of even more content, all of which will contribute towards our Digital Tattoos. We, as users, need to take back control of our data, how it's being used and by whom – before someone else does.

When it comes to the state of our Online Reputation, many of us have work to to do, mainly because we've given little or no thought to what we've created in the past, i.e. the stuff that's yet to come back to haunt us (our digital skeletons in the closet).

With the growth of Social Media over the past few years, many of us have turned to platforms such as Twitter to search for information – social searches will play a massive part in our Online Reputation in addition to what appears in search engines, and we'll also need to worry about what's appearing when we carry out a search on Twitter or Facebook for example. A lot of the time, it's difficult to control what others post or share about us via social media platforms. But we need to be aware of this risk and take steps to limit any damage it can cause. Once information goes online, it stays online and it's difficult to near impossible to remove all trace of it.

One thing for sure is that gossip and rumour will continue to abound online. The Internet and Social Media provides a real time channel for it to be accessed – on speed dial, should one wish. As in 'real life', gossip and rumour can cause a lot of damage and the ramifications can be disastrous, especially now that each and every of us has the opportunity to connect with and create an endless supply of digital content.

We're becoming ever more connected and will continue to do so. I mean, even newborn babies have a digital footprint. Scrap that – even before they're born they have a Digital Tattoo. 'But Wayne', I hear you say, 'how can they get a Digital Tattoo in the womb?' Well, the 12 week scan for a start. Many parents post this online – normally on Facebook for family and friends to see. Maybe in the future there'll be an app for this – who knows.

Soon the technology will be everywhere and we'll be able to share where we are, what we're doing and how we're feeling – maybe even unwittingly from the technology we wear.

I've learned a lot over the past 18 years using the internet daily, becoming a prolific social networker and launching Ireland's first Social Network Website. Yes I can remember that awful dial up sound and AOL screaming 'You've got mail'. Times have changed so much for the better with technology.

The tools and the technology have played, and will continue to play, an important part in my life. Before the Interwebs, if I wanted to learn about anything new, I'd have had to dig out a massive Encyclopaedia Britannica. Anyway, I'll bet I could look information up online a lot quicker than it takes to win the bid on eBay and get it shipped to where I live. That's how much stuff has changed in just 18 years.

I hope this book has highlighted the amazing opportunities which Social Media, the Internet and our new digital technology provides on a daily basis for us to take advantage of – and believe me, I do take advantage of it! I've been lucky enough to create opportunities largely as a result of using the tools I've been discussing in this book. I've been able to travel to the USA, Middle East and soon, Australia to speak to young people, parents, educators and businesses about protecting and managing their Online Reputation. Something I may not have thought possible when I was a teenager.

I've been able to build relationships with my peers in other countries and cultures. I've had global brands headhunt me for senior roles, in fact, built roles around me. I've had Marketing and Media outlets contact me to speak on TV and Radio from Boston to Dubai on aspects of online reputation... and you know what? I'm only scratching the surface of what's yet to come in terms of my career. I've built a successful personal brand around my Digital Ninja blogs, receiving thousands of visitors per month... [That's enough showing off, Ed.]

I'm not (just ☺) saying these things to boast, I'm telling you this because if I can do it, you can. You can use the internet and social networking to rock your world.

None of this has been easy. In fact, it's required lots of hard work and effort. Mainly by me. But others have helped a little along the way ☺. By being key players in online and mobile influencing making the internet a better place to be. Look at the great things that are being accomplished and how others use technology as a force for good.

You see, I believe being positive online breeds positivity and reduces negativity and mis-use. And you know what – it's contagious. It infects others along the way, so much so that they want to connect and work with you. Your voice online can have incredible power and used in the correct way online, I have found, can open up fantastic opportunities and reach further than you dreamed of... if directed at the right audience. You need to know your audience, your platform or channel and how it can be used to maximum effect – no half-ass approach allowed.

To get a return, you have to put in the effort. You need to spend the time building your network of connections and creating content which people want to read. Content is the key to growing your network but it needs to be created with thought, knowledge and insight.

STOP I THINK I POST

/YOLO
The platforms which we all have access to today offer much more than just a soapbox for us to vent our frustrations about daily life – don't be one of those ranters. Your time is too precious.

To get value and the kind of return that could take you and your life to a place you can only dream off, you'll need to make an investment in yourself, which includes your increasingly important Digital Self.

That's how you'll get ahead in today's world, and that's how your future will be shaped. It's up to you.

THE END

TOP TIP
If I can do it, you can. You can use the internet and social networking to rock your world.

REFERENCES

1. FB Source - http://www.businessinsider.com/facebook-350-million-photos-each-day-2013-9 and http://expandedramblings.com/index.php/by-the-numbers-17-amazing-facebook-stats/#.UuPaPWTFJsM

2. http://www.techopedia.com/definition/29591/online-reputation-management-orm

3. (Time: http://business.time.com/2012/07/09/how-recruiters-use-social-networks-to-make-hiring-decisions-now/)

4. http://mashable.com/2011/10/23/how-recruiters-use-social-networks-to-screen-candidates-infographic/

5. http://www.mediabistro.com/alltwitter/uk-top-mobile-apps_b58995

6. http://www.reputationmanagement.com/hiring-managers-care-online-reputation/

7. http://ec.europa.eu/digital-agenda/en/grand-coalition-digital-jobs

8. http://press.linkedin.com/about

9. [add to references section http://press.linkedin.com/about.]

10. http://www.time-to-change.org.uk/sites/default/files/TTC%20CYP%20Report%20FINAL.pdf

11. http://www.coolinfographics.com/blog/2012/6/15/200-infographic-resumes-an-escalating-trend.html

12. http://newsfeed.time.com/2013/06/12/surprise-narcissism-linked-to-

frequent-facebook-and-twitter-use/

13. http://digitaljournal.com/article/352294

14. http://www.huffingtonpost.com/2012/07/17/burger-king-employee-steps-in-lettuce-busted-4chan_n_1679793.html

15. http://www.theguardian.com/technology/2012/mar/17/facebook-dark-side-study-aggressive-narcissism

16. *Cisco's 2012 analysis of global mobile data traffic* http://www.cisco.com/c/en/us/solutions/collateral/service-provider/visual-networking-index-vni/white_paper_c11-520862.html

17. http://www.bbc.co.uk/news/world-europe-27388289

18. http://www.nytimes.com/2014/05/14/technology/google-should-erase-web-links-to-some-personal-data-europes-highest-court-says.html?_r=0

19. http://www.theguardian.com/sport/2013/mar/12/english-boxer-curtis-woodhouse-twitter-troll

20. https://www.jobvite.com/wp-content/uploads/2014/10/Jobvite_SocialRecruiting_Survey2014.pdf

21. http://metro.co.uk/2015/07/21/deportivo-la-coruna-cancel-striker-transfer-after-discovering-he-abused-club-on-twitter-in-2012-5305262/

22. http://m.thedrum.com/knowledge-bank/2012/10/29/footballers-shown-red-card-tweeting-faux-pas

Acknowledgments

This has been no easy task. If you had asked me a few years ago if I would ever have been able to sit down and write a book I would have said you were barking mad…

The support which I've received from a bunch of close people who I call my family and friends have been the inspiration to make it happen and for that I'm going to single you guys out ☺

Elaine - Your belief and immense support in everything I do - this book and other projects would not have been possible. 3.8.1

Charlie & Jonny - Each day you both give me a new reason to smile and push forward. We won't mention the constant distractions namely bug hunting and football...

» Mary Commins - For just always being there. Thanks Mum ☺

» Kevin McAllister - For showing me the ropes in PR and helping me get the message out on the Wireless

» Rowan Hand – For giving me a chance in the early days.

» Frank McKee – For giving me a start in front of an audience

» Andrew Brodigan - For not listening when others once did

» Madaleine McCrink - For believing in the message

» Valda Mikalauskaite – Your awesomeness

» Tracey Edwards MBE – For telling me I was on the right page

» Connaire McCreevy – For highlighting cybersafety in the local community

- » Scott Richie - Now it's your turn Sir James

- » Jonathan Kenna, Sarah Wragg & Paul McDonnell - For getting this to the finish

- » Barry Lee Cummins - The only other Digital Ninja I know

- » Simon Clegg – My speaking brother, our skype calls are always great inspiration

- » Marc Montgomery - For buying the first copy of this book ☺

- » Sam - Even though you can't talk back I know you are always listening

Lastly and most importantly the children, young people, parents, educators and professionals who I've had the pleasure to meet and learn from when delivering my talks and to whom this book is dedicated.

ABOUT THE AUTHOR

Wayne is a Speaker, Author, Trainer & Entrepreneur

He motivates and inspires thousands of Young People, Parents and Educators delivering the Online Reputation Matters Program to schools in the UK, Ireland and the Middle East. Wayne is an award winning Entrepreneur who helps businesses protect and improve their Online Reputation in a rapidly changing digital world. He is a regular commentator for media outlets such as BBC and UTV and advises government, voluntary and charitable organisations on cybersafety and the impact of social media.

Wayne helps empower young people to use social media more responsibly, protect their Online Reputation and become more employable and helps businesses to stay ahead of the game.

Printed in Great
Britain
by Amazon